CW01506589

The R.F.C. in the Great War

Royal Flying Corps Uniform and Badges

The R.F.C. in the Great War

Pilots, Organisation, Activities and Actions, 1914-18

ILLUSTRATED

The Royal Flying Corps in the War
"Wing Adjutant"

War in the Air Tales
A. G. Hales, H. Harper, M. Pemberton

LEONAUR

The R.F.C. in the Great War
Pilots, Organisation, Activities and Actions, 1914-18
The Royal Flying Corps in the War
by "Wing Adjutant"
War in the Air Tales
A. G. Hales, H. Harper, M. Pemberton

ILLUSTRATED

FIRST EDITION

Leonaur is an imprint of Oakpast Ltd

Copyright in this form © 2022 Oakpast Ltd

ISBN: 978-1-915234-16-2 (hardcover)
ISBN: 978-1-915234-17-9 (softcover)

http://www.leonaur.com

Publisher's Notes

The views expressed in this book are not necessarily
those of the publisher.

Contents

Preface

Of all the tales and sketches which go to make up the present work, some have been actual experiences of the writer, more of other members of the Royal Flying Corps, whilst one or two are purely imaginative, but none the less possible.

In cases where the writer may seem to be inaccurate or out of date, he begs to remind his readers that the sketches were written in the autumn of 1916, in most instances, and portray events as they happened to him and his contemporaries in the R.F.C., mostly in 1915, and the beginning of 1916. After that date the writer ceased to fly himself, owing to a period of eight months in hospital, and became a "Wing Adjutant." The details of the R.F.C. in the East were obtained whilst he was actually there during the greater part of 1917.

W. T. B.

CHAPTER 1

The Call of the Air

"When one has spent weary hours in England, shouting oneself hoarse in efforts to instruct dull-witted recruits to know their right hands from their left, more smeary hours trapesing through muddy English fields and lanes, and yet more hours digging trenches in all sorts of conditions from hot and dry to wet with the rain freezing stiff as it fell, one has the right to expect better than this."

So thought Lieut. B—— as he lay in his bed in Blighty—only it wasn't called Blighty then. That was a term to come later on in the war; at that early date, late in 1914, the now familiar word was more or less unknown, and public controversy, instead, raged strongly around the derivation of the words "gone West," some declaring them to be taken from a popular song, others babbling of mythological folk-lore and the Islands of the Hesperides.

All this scarcely concerned Lieut. B——, for he was not "gone West." Nor was there the smallest chance of his going to that delectable region, for he was merely confined to bed with the slightest possible of wounds, and the prospect of a speedy return to France and all the drudgery of infantry work and trench warfare. Too speedy; for as he had been thinking, he expected better than this. In other words, after a short but horrible nightmare period of infantry work, of which a confused jumble of noise, stench, water, grey uniforms and mud—chiefly mud—were his chief memories, he wished for a change, and set about thinking what could be done to obtain it.

The only possible thing to do was to transfer to some entirely different unit—some unit, if possible, where such things as mud ceased to trouble, and yet where one would not be altogether "out of it." The Gunners were asking for more officers, but artillery work did not appeal to him; the A.S.C. was quite out of the question, even if they'd have had him, which he doubted; cavalry work is too much as infantry these days. What was to be done? And then as he lay there it dawned upon him. Why not try the R.F.C.?

Why not indeed? He had some flying experience and certain qualifications, and the work seemed good. Often, he had watched the white ships go sailing over, tiny specks in the blue, miles over his head, their serenity seemingly unruffled by the angry little puffs of smoke bursting around them. The pilots were out of the sickening stench of the trenches, and had the chance of individual shows against the enemy. True, the danger was great—not only was there the Hun to contend with, but all the forces of Nature to reckon against—but the game seemed good. He had no one at home to worry about, and there was the prospect of unlimited adventure ten thousand feet in the air, and chances of rapid promotion. Already he could feel the tug of the control lever, and hear the roar of the engine.

That very day his application for a transfer to the R.F.C. went in, and he began to await events.

Time went by and he rejoined his depot. Once again came the dull task of training those hopeless recruits who eventually make the best finished article in the world. Once more he tramped through muddy lanes, once more he swore, chilled to the bone, as the men dug trenches—it was early in 1915—and still he heard nothing from the War Office.

Impatience caused the request to the adjutant to send in a reminder, but that officer advised patience, and next day came the awaited letter. Its contents were brief, and the lieutenant was little further forward with his transfer. Still, he had to attend at the War Office at his convenience, and there be interviewed as to his fitness for the Corps. Needless to say, it was not many days before he presented himself at the offices of the D.A.O.—how familiar those letters afterwards became—(for the uninitiated I may translate them as Directorate of Air Organisation), and with many fears filled in his slip, and was escorted by a small boy scout to a seat at the end of a row of others—civilians and soldiers alike—all awaiting their turn with the same object as himself.

After what seemed many aeons (it was only an hour and a half really), during which newcomers were constantly being added to the list, his name was called, and he entered the presence of the one whom he had to satisfy as to his fitness to become a member of the Corps which heads the Army List. This officer proceeded to question him as to many things, and, finally, to his great relief, remarked that he would do, and as he seemed to have special qualifications he would endeavour to hurry him through.

He returned to his regiment, and again commenced to wait. With that last promise still in his ears he daily expected orders telling him to report somewhere or other to take up his new duties, but the weeks passed by, and eventually the battalion was moved to Salisbury Plain, and with it himself. As if out of sheer cussedness, no sooner had the move taken place than one morning the expected order came.

While lying with his platoon in the shelter of some bushes, some miles away from camp, a breathless figure approached, saluted, and gasped out that the adjutant wanted him in the Orderly Room at once—with more than ordinary speed it seemed—so he set out at the double, well guessing what was in store for him. No sooner did he arrive than a railway warrant and telegram were thrust into his hand, and he was told to rush to the station and catch the train forthwith. His baggage was packed and waiting, and with this short notice he was wrung by the hand, wished good luck, and pushed off to his new job. Once in the train he had time to read the telegram:

Instruct Lieut. B—— to report H—— forthwith for instruction in aviation.

He had got his transfer; it remained to be seen what he would do with it.

CHAPTER 2

Training

To be accepted by the War Office as a candidate for the Royal Flying Corps does not mean that the applicant is already a member of the elect. He has a very long and arduous course of training to go through, and many men have to return to their regiments, generally through no fault of their own, but simply because they are unfitted to the strenuous work of a pilot in the R.F.C. Though I speak of the training of a pilot, he being the actual flying man and the senior class of the Corps, it must not be supposed that the Air Service is composed solely of flying men. I do not think I am far wrong in saying that only about a half of the officers are actually pilots, and of the men only an infinitesimally small proportion ever go up in an aeroplane, and a still smaller number actually become pilots.

To each aeroplane a crew of two riggers and two fitters is allotted. They may be either 1st or 2nd A.M.s (air mechanics). Riggers look after the fabric, wiring, woodwork and general exterior of the machine, whilst the fitters are responsible for the condition and running of the engine. Other men work on an aeroplane as occasion arises—carpenters, sailmakers, &c.; blacksmiths, tinsmiths, instrument repairers, and men of countless other trades are in attendance to see to the ailments of engine, instruments, or any other of the delicate parts of the anatomy of an aeroplane. There are also drivers of cars and lorries, riders of motorcycles, wireless telegraphists, storemen, and clerks galore. So much for the men; I will speak of their actual work later.

Officers are roughly of three classes—pilots, observers and equipment officers (not including the Kite-Balloon Sections), and before giving a detailed description of the training of a pilot—as the most representative "class" in the R.F.C.—a few words regarding the others may help to a better understanding of the Corps.

Observers, as their name implies, fly with the pilot, but their work consists of a great deal more than observing only. The observer is a trained wireless operator; he is an expert at photography under difficulties; he is a crack shot, and understands thoroughly the intricacies of machine-guns; he is a man of iron nerve and unblenching courage—in fact, he is a compendium of all the special branches of the army, and second only to the pilot in expert knowledge. The majority of observers eventually train as pilots, and they are, naturally, with their double training, amongst the best men in the Corps.

To train a pilot takes many weeks, and often costs many pounds. After selection by the War Office, the candidate, whom we may now designate the pupil, is sent on to one or other of the training schools, and it depends very largely on the pupil's adaptability as to the time that it takes for him to be passed out of the School of Instruction and actually commence flying. At the end of the course, he is examined in all the subjects in which he has been under instruction. Needless to say, these are many and varied, and it says much for the skill of the instructors—N.C.O.'s and officers—that such good results are obtained in such a short time.

Engines alone—one of the most important subjects—would baffle the average learner, but such is the keenness displayed by both instructors and pupils that a working knowledge of rigging aeroplanes, theory of flight, wireless, cross-country flying, map reading, meteorology, the construction of bombs and machine-guns, aerial photography, and countless other subjects is acquired during this short course.

A visit to the instructional engine-rooms reveals numbers of small groups of dungaree-clad figures occupied in dismantling a Gnome or Beardmore, or industriously taking notes from a grimy, oil-stained instructor. The rigging-sheds contain skeletons of many types of machines in varying stages of construction, and here again the dungaree-clad groups build and splice and measure and take notes. Not a figure is slacking; everyone is intent on his work and hard at it. From the rigging-sheds visit the test benches, where engines, fitted with their propellers are roaring out their revolutions in varying notes for the benefit of the pupils, who thus learn how to tune up an engine and judge by the sound if it is running properly.

The bomb-room, with its examples of all weights, from the baby 20 lb. to the giant 500 lb. engine of destruction, is the place where pupils are taught to fit the fuses with safety to themselves and danger to the foe, and in the same room may usually be found the Lewis gun—the chief weapon of almost every British aeroplane. Sounds of buzzing proclaim the room where Morse and wireless are taught, and other rooms receive classes for instruction in subjects which bewilder the beginner, but soon get him in their grip, so that he learns at least the elements of his work.

At the end of six weeks the pupil sits to a written examination. If he should fail in a single subject, he takes the whole course again, but if he passes—and the high standard of 60 *per cent*, is required for a pass—he is sent on to an aerodrome for instruction in aviation. It is here that the beginner's weak points are quickly found.

On first joining up at the aerodrome the pupil generally has to wait a while before he gets his first flight, as, somewhat naturally, the instructors have their pupils whom they wish to push on to the solo stage before commencing with a newcomer. The instructors are usually officers who have done their bit at the front and have been sent home for a rest. The hours during which a pupil waits for his first flight are not wasted, for he may learn a lot from watching the movements of machines in the air and from the remarks of his more advanced companions. He thus learns that it is bad to climb while turning, and he can quickly notice a bad take-off or landing. When the time eventually comes for him to make his first flight, he does very little; indeed, he merely sits in the passenger seat, and looks round whilst the instructor gives him a "joy ride" in order that he may learn what it feels like to be in the air. These first flights often lead a pupil to discover he has nerves; and then unless he wishes to rejoin his regiment, he is usually permitted to become an equipment officer or join the Kite-Balloon Section.

Provided his first flight comes off all right—and it is rather a weird experience that first flight—he now commences to receive proper instruction, and gradually any strangeness he may feel in his new element passes away. At first, he merely places his hands and feet on the controls—all instructional machines are fitted with dual control—and feels the various movements made by the instructor in climbing, descending and turning; but later he will gradually commence to make the movements himself, and, probably without knowing it, fly the machine himself.

Then a system of signals is generally arranged between pilot and pupil; usually, if the instructor is in front, he raises his right hand if he wishes the pupil to take control, and his left when he wishes to take

Officers of the Royal Flying Corps

over control again himself. In this way the pupil knows that he is actually, at times, flying the aeroplane himself, and he realises his mistakes as he feels the instructor correct them.

When the pupil is fairly confident whilst actually in the air, he is allowed to take control of the engine when the machine is on the ground, "taxi" it after it has landed, and then at last take the machine into the air. He is not yet allowed to land the machine. These two actions of flying are left to the last because it is in them solely that the danger and difficulty of aviation lie. When rising, a careless pilot may easily climb too quickly, or try to rise before the machine has gained sufficient speed, and thus "stall" (come down tail first) or side-slip the aeroplane when he has not sufficient altitude in which to recover, but has ample in which to crash both the machine and himself.

Similarly, when descending, an inexperienced pilot may dive the machine too steeply, and crash into the ground before he is able to flatten out; he may come down at an insufficiently steep angle and stall the machine; he may "pancake" (flop down in a heap) through flattening out too early, or misjudge his landing and run into an obstacle. Small wonder, the, that the instructor makes very sure of his pupil before he allows him to take off or land a machine. Taking off is not difficult, and only needs care; and the pupil is then allowed to feel the motions made by the pilot in landing—throttle back the engine, depress the control lever, a long smooth glide, and then a flattening out by raising the lever, and the machine is safely landed.

Up to this time the pupil has sat in the passenger seat, but at this point he is usually promoted to that of the pilot and with average ability is soon able to land the machine safely without any help from the instructor. He is now ready for his greatest ordeal—the first solo flight. Instructors make very sure of their pupils before they allow them to fly alone, and choose a day free from wind and bumps for their first flight.

At last, the novice is strapped in alone, told to fly once round the aerodrome and land—a trying test for the best of nerves. With a rush of wind and a roar of the engine the pupil goes off, and the instructor remains watching as anxiously as a hen whose chicks have taken to water. Slowly the aeroplane circles, and at last, with a diminution of noise, dips its nose to land. This is the supreme test; perhaps the pupil forgets to flatten out, and crashes badly; he may pancake, or just make an ordinary bad landing in which the machine touches land with a bump, and goes flying over the ground like a kangaroo in a Marathon race before finally coming to rest.

In any of these cases the pupil receives more instruction in landing, until he at last flies easily and well. He is then ready to take his "ticket"—the certificate of the *Fédération Aéronautique Internationale*. Up to this time—if he is an average pilot—he has had about three and a half hours' actual flying, split up into odd five and ten minutes in the air.

In order to take a "ticket" a pilot has to pass three tests. He first has to fly solo in five figures of eight, this involving right and left-hand turns, and finally stop on landing within fifty yards of a given mark. He then has to ascend and repeat the performance; and finally, rising a third time to a height of over 350 feet, he must switch off his engine and make a volplane or glide to earth. Should all these tests be passed to the satisfaction of the official witnesses, a form is filled in and sent up to the Royal Aero Club, together with a cheque, and in due course the pupil becomes a certified aviator, qualified to fly at exhibitions and race meetings, and a person of no small importance in his own eyes. But he has yet a long way to go before he graduates as a flying officer of the R.F.C.

Shortly after taking his ticket, the pupil probably commences to fly a new type of machine, for the man who can only fly one aeroplane is of little use in the service. The same process is gone through with the new machine as when learning to fly, but, needless to say, it takes the novice less time to master his second machine than it does the first. About this time, too, short cross-country flights are undertaken solo by the pupil, for up till now his efforts have been confined to circling round the aerodrome. A third type of machine soon follows, and the cross-country flights increase in length and difficulty. No longer is the pilot told to follow a certain well-marked route, but he is given a map and told to make the circuit of certain towns.

His flights are timed, and should he exceed the time that the instructor knows the flight should properly take, inquiries are instituted on his return as to why and where he lost himself, for every yard flown should be followed on the map—exact compass reckoning is impossible in the air on account of drift and the attraction of the various metal fittings of the aeroplane. Probably during one of these flights the pilot will have trouble with his engine and be forced to land in strange country. Woe be to him if he has failed to keep a possible spot for landing constantly within reach.

This is one of the first principles of cross-country flying. This forced landing tests the pupil's knowledge of his engine; should the fault be a simple one he must repair it himself, and provided he has landed safely, and can find someone to start up his engine, proceed with his journey. Should the engine or machine he badly damaged, the pilot must wire for help and guard his machine until he is relieved.

At last, when he can fly several types of machines satisfactorily, and find his way about strange country with ease, the instructor reports on his progress to the Wing Commander, and that officer, either taking the instructor's word or examining the pupil's flying himself, gives a certificate to the effect that the pupil is proficient in flying and cross-country flying, and, in his opinion, fit to graduate as a flying officer.

In a few days a graduation certificate arrives, and the pupil is now a pupil no longer, but may wear the double wings of the flying officer. (The course of training has now undergone various alterations, but the principles remain the same.—W. T. B.) Up to this time he has probably had from twenty-five to thirty hours actually in the air, and is now well qualified for work overseas or in any other capacity.

It may be as well to state that in the early days of the war pupils did not receive this dual course of instruction, but commenced aviation straightaway, and picked up their knowledge of engines, rigging, &c., in the intervals of flying, and despite these difficulties, passed a practical examination quite up to the standard of the present elaborate affair.

All honour to those early pilots who gained such an astonishing ascendancy over the foe, and honour, too, to those younger members of the Corps who have maintained it.

CHAPTER 3

The Long Reconnaissance

When a pilot is posted to the Expeditionary Force, he may pro-ceed overseas with a new squadron which is going out for the first time, or he may proceed alone to replace a casualty in one of the squadrons already in the field. Needless to say, most officers prefer to go out with a squadron among men whom they know well, but even with the Corps at its present huge dimensions, one cannot be for long in it without knowing a large proportion of the total personnel, for changes are continually taking place and new faces constantly met.

It is almost impossible to visit any squadron without meeting at least one or two well-known faces, and it is largely this point of gen-eral acquaintance which is responsible for the *esprit de corps*. Needless to say, squadrons indulge in friendly rivalry, and the competition is great to see who can bring down the largest number of Huns; this is only natural, and as it should be.

One of the most disliked, and at the same time inevitable, of the tasks of the R.F.C. is the long reconnaissance—a flight of three or four hours many miles behind the enemy's lines, and a task calling for the greatest skill, powers of endurance, and devotion to duty. A new pilot usually has time to get his local bearings pretty thoroughly before his turn arrives for this piece of work, and then one day his squadron commander will tell him to take his machine and an observer, and thoroughly reconnoitre a certain area. In the summer the task is not so bad, but a three or four hours' flight in the depth of winter at an altitude of many thousand feet is not a job to be sought after.

Pilot and observer both muffle themselves up in sweaters and thick leather coats, an extra pair of socks and fur-lined knee boots are donned, a woollen balaclava is worn under the fur-lined helmet, scarves are wrapped round the neck to exclude all possible draught, a leather mask fitted with goggles is worn to protect the face, for the intense cold often causes frostbite and the most ghastly mutilations of the features, and, lastly, big fur gauntlets are pulled on well up to the elbow.

Maps, notebooks, pencils are collected, bombs are placed on the bomb ribs, drums of ammunition are brought to feed the machine-gun with which to beat off pugnacious Huns, a camera is sometimes fitted to its rack, the tanks are filled with oil and petrol, and, finally, the pilot having had a last inspection of his machine, both he and the observer strap themselves in, the pilot cries "Contact," and with a roar the big propeller commences to revolve. Slowly it swings at first, then faster and faster, and at length, the engine being well warmed up to its work, slows down again. The pilot waves his arm, waiting mechanics pull the chocks from under the wheels, the propeller again gains speed, and the aeroplane rushes over the ground, and up in ever higher circles until sufficient altitude has been reached, when a course is steered to the line.

On these flights it is the observer who is in command. He lets the pilot know where he wants to fly, directs him to right or left, causes him to circle over any spot which he wishes specially to observe, and generally directs operations. Though these reconnaissances are not made with offensive purposes, bombs are carried in case a good target should suddenly appear—a large body of troops in the open, a big convoy on the road, or several trains in a station.

Similarly, a machine-gun is carried for defensive purposes, and though the pilot on one of these flights should rather avoid than seek a fight, it is perhaps unnecessary to say that should a Boche machine appear with the object of driving our machine away or preventing its reaching the objective, pilot and observer between them always manage to put up a good fight, and it is usually the Hun who retires discomfited.

When fighting, the pilot commands the aeroplane and manoeuvres as he thinks fit, both he and his observer using their machine-guns as opportunity offers. Needless to say, it is absolutely essential that both officers have complete confidence in themselves and each other, and that differences of opinion do not exist between them. For this reason, the same pair generally work together, and a perfect understanding soon reigns between them.

Once over the trenches, which are usually crossed at a height of anything over 8,000 feet, the work of the day begins. As a rule, orders are given to look for some special object, or thoroughly reconnoitre a special area, often a hundred miles behind the lines, though generally the whole of a large area has to be surveyed, and all enemy movements and positions of parks, gun emplacements, &c., noted. Generally, the pilot arranges with his observer beforehand the route to be flown over, so that the whole area can be thoroughly covered.

Stations, railway junctions, suspected ammunition dumps, new aerodromes, and possible gun emplacements are all subjected to scrutiny, and from time to time the observer thrusts his hand through an aperture in the palm of his gauntlet in order to note an unusual number of trains in a station, or the exact location on the map of any point of special interest.

Occasionally a station may be reached as troops are detraining or a large convoy may be seen on the road. Then, if "Archie" is not too active, or if the pilot be particularly daring, the aeroplane will rapidly dive through space until close enough for the pilot to make sure of his target, when two or three bombs are dropped, to the discomfort of the Hun. A puff of smoke, perhaps the faint boom of the explosion, and scattering troops or an overturned lorry let the pilot know that his shots have taken effect, and that it is time to quit before things get too hot for him.

These little affairs do little real damage to material, but they are of immense effect in destroying the German morale. The mere fact that British machines can and do venture so far over enemy territory has done a lot towards intimidating Fritz, and causing him to christen the Corps with many uncomplimentary names—in truth a real compliment to the efficiency of the R.F.C.

It may be the emplacement of a huge howitzer, or a large dump of stores and ammunition, of which the observer signifies his wish to see more, and the pilot must circle and dodge, first turning this way, then climbing that way, diving a few hundred feet—in fact, employing all the tricks of his trade in order to dodge those devilish puffs of smoke which burst now here, now there, now so close that it seems the next must hit, but when it comes the pilot has left it well away to the right.

Possibly a few stray holes appear in the fabric of the wings, but so long as a main spar is not broken, a control wire severed, or the engine damaged, all is well, and the game of touch continues. Meanwhile the observer has been peering at the ground, utterly unconcerned by the flying shells—they are all in the day's work—or the queer positions taken by the machine as the pilot dodges hither and thither. At last, he finds what he is looking for, marks it carefully on the map, possibly photographs it, and eventually gives the signal for the pilot to carry on with the journey.

So, the day proceeds, until every inch of the ground has been covered and the machine heads for home. As the line is approached the danger again increases, and often, whilst the pilot is engaged in dodging the "Archies," suddenly out of the clouds darts an enemy machine, diving hawk-like on its adversary. A few shots are generally exchanged before the Hun—having missed the object of his wild dive—sheers off, the usual ending to these little affairs. Once safely over the lines the pilot begins to descend until his aerodrome is reached, where he lands in safety.

Both he and his observer are stiff with the cold—in the winter it is often necessary to help them out of the machine and attend to the chilled parts of the body in order to avoid frostbite—their faces are drawn with the severe strain, they are deaf from the continual roar of the engine, their eyes are bloodshot, and their whole bodies are racked with every imaginable ache. For the next few hours, they are good for nothing but rest, though sleep usually refuses to comfort their overstrained minds; but before turning in the observer must make out his report, and hand it in to the proper quarters. It is good that the long reconnaissance comes seldom, for no one could stand a continual strain of these wearying flights.

Many incidents happen which prove the saying that truth is stranger than fiction, and though some of the stories told of the R.F.C. are distinctly efforts on the part of somebody's imagination, many true happenings read like fiction. The following is an example:

While on the long reconnaissance, and many miles behind the German line, Lieuts. A. and B.—both of them pilots, though B. was acting as observer—had the luck to encounter a Boche machine miles from its aerodrome or any antiaircraft station. What the Hun was doing here no one knows—probably flying from a base to one of their aerodromes—but without hesitation Lieut. A. flew at the enemy, manoeuvred for position, and when nicely under his tail Lieut. B. opened fire with the machine-gun.

The Boche had little chance to retaliate, being outmanoeuvred and singlehanded, and presently dived steeply, followed by the British machine. He was seen to land safely in an out-of-the-way spot with his propeller stopped, and the British aeroplane circled overhead, waiting to see what would happen. The pilot did not attempt to get out, and the machine remained where it was; so, Lieut. A., seeing that there were no houses near, and little likelihood of any of the enemy being in the vicinity, decided to land beside his silent foe and investigate matters. He planed down and landed, Lieut. B. meanwhile keeping the Boche covered with his machine-gun in case of any tricks.

A. stopped his engine and, together with B., both armed with revolvers, advanced towards the other aeroplane. Nothing happened, and on investigation they discovered that during the short fight in the air one of B.'s bullets had hit the Hun airman, cutting a vein, and he had bled to death, just living long enough to reach the earth. His machine was intact and his tanks full, so it did not take A. and B. long to decide what to do. A. kept to his own machine, and B. took the Hun "'bus." They started up each other's engines, got off in safety, and set out for the British lines. Despite heavy shelling on the part of our anti-aircraft guns, who naturally thought it a raiding Boche, Lieut. B. successfully brought the captured machine home, and landed it in his own aerodrome, much to the surprise of his fellow officers, who were astonished at this seemingly strange action on the part of the enemy.

On another occasion the observer, who was sitting in front of the pilot, was surprised at the queer behaviour of the machine. Despite heavy shelling by "Archie," the pilot seemed to be holding a dead straight course—the most dangerous thing to do under the circumstances. When the observer—Lieut. C.—turned round to remonstrate with the pilot he found that gentleman hanging forward in his seat, with the blood trickling from a wound in his head. He had evidently been hit by shrapnel, and the aeroplane, being of an automatically stable type, left without his controlling hand, had carried on straight ahead. This would continue until the petrol gave out, or until "Archie" who was creeping nearer and nearer, obtained a good hit and damaged the engine or some other vital part, then a long steep dive, and a sickening crash, and all would be over.

It did not take C. long to realise this, or to make up his mind as to what action to take. Leaving his seat he crawled from it over to the dead pilot's place; but no sooner was he there than the additional weight aft of the centre of gravity caused the machine gradually to drop her tail, lose flying speed, stall, and tail-dive for some hundreds of feet.

Luckily for C. all this occurred at an altitude of many thousands of feet; and, seated on the body of his pilot, he proceeded to correct

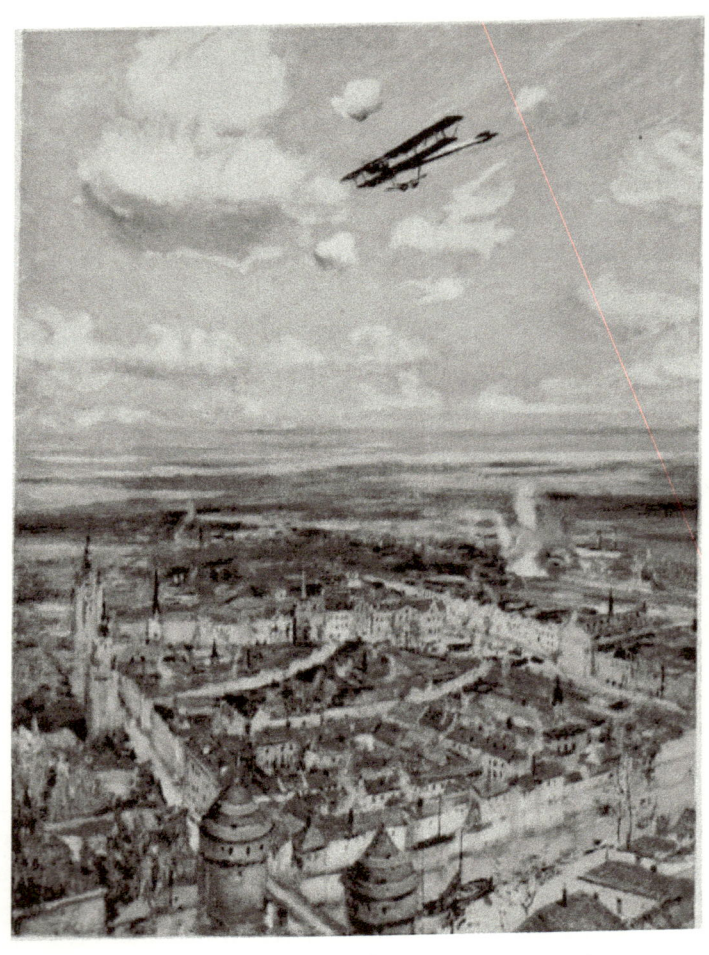

LIEUTENANT RHODES-MOORHOUSE FLYING OVER COURTRAI
TO BOMB THE RAILWAY

the machine. Observers naturally know what actions to go through to fly an aeroplane. Also, the machine in question was stable, and, despite the disturbance of the balance, only needed guiding, so that C. managed to gain control and fly over the lines, and though he did not land safely, he did so without damage to himself.

Sometimes queer mistakes are made whilst on reconnaissance, not only by us but by the enemy, who on one occasion made us the present of a brand-new machine complete with pilot and observer.

It happened in this way.

At one of our aerodromes in France about 3 o'clock in the morning the officer on duty, happening to be awake, heard the sound of an aeroplane engine, and knowing that none of the machines of his own particular squadron was out at that hour, turned out in his pyjamas to see what was happening. He was just in time to see an aeroplane descend, misjudge its landing, and sail off again. The type of machine was unfamiliar to him, and his suspicions were aroused.

Also the machine, dimly seen in the faint, grey light, seemed in doubt whether to attempt another landing or not. Eventually the pilot fired a signal. Lieut. D. hastily, in his turn, fired a signal light. That seemed to satisfy the occupants of the machine, who circled with the evident intention of landing, Lieut. D. immediately got a revolver, called out the guard, and awaited events.

The aeroplane glided smoothly along, and as it landed the waiting party could dimly distinguish the black cross painted on the planes. As soon as it came to a stop Lieut. D., covering it himself and backed by an armed guard, called on the occupants to surrender. They evidently thought discretion the better part of valour, and held up their hands. They were disarmed, allowed to leave their machine, and placed under guard.

Lieut. D. then went to inform his Squadron Commander that he had just captured two Huns and a brand-new aeroplane—this in his pyjamas at 3 a.m. Practical jokes are, somewhat naturally, rather prevalent in the Corps, and the major, very irate at being awakened at such an hour, thought this to be one, and angrily bade his subaltern withdraw. The latter, however, stuck to his statement, and a very amazed major arose to interview his two captives. They had been on a job involving night flying, and on returning had lost their bearing in the morning mist, taken the aerodrome for their own, and attempted to land. The machine proved to be quite new, and when flown back to England was found to possess several gadgets of great use and interest.

CHAPTER 4

All in the Day's Work

Aloft in the single-seated fighter the pilot has steadily beaten from end to end of the allotted line he is patrolling for the best part of two hours, keeping a keen look-out for any enemy airman who dares to approach, but until now the horizon has been clear.

Down below him stretch the flat plains of Flanders, dotted with tiny villages and solitary farmsteads that, from his elevation of 8,000 feet, seem to lie in peaceful seclusion. At one point he can see a number of tiny dots which move with the restless activity of so many ants—an enemy engineer working-party. In the distance the smoke of trains shows at various points, and a regular column of insects moving slowly along one of the long, straight roads betrays troops being moved from one point to another.

Beside and below him, and some few miles off—for he is flying the German side of the line whilst patrolling—are the long, jagged cuts, or series of cuts, contorting themselves over endless miles until they are lost to sight in either direction, where countless millions of many nationalities are striving for the mastery. There is no sign of life there, for all is quiet on this sector. No flashes betray the position of ill-hidden guns, and not the faintest rumble of concentrated thunder reaches the pilot as he soars some mile and a half above the earth. Even "Archie" is silent for a while, though he has been busy during the afternoon.

Suddenly he sees a speck in the distance, which gradually grows larger until at last it resolves itself into a slow-moving biplane, one of a type seldom seen unescorted by a fast fighting aeroplane to protect it. The pilot of the British machine watches it carefully. It is so far away that, should he attempt to attack, the enemy could fly off long before he gets within effective range of his Lewis gun.

TYPES OF GERMANY'S LONG-DISTANCE BOMBING MACHINES

Without warning, a puff of smoke appears in front of him, another behind, and a third close at his side. Automatically, as the explosions cause his machine to rock violently, he puts down the nose of his machine, banks her over steeply, and spirals down some hundreds of feet to put "Archie" off the track. As the shells descend to his level, and commence to burst around him, he puts his nose down slightly and rushes along at terrific speed, suddenly zooming up almost perpendicularly and darting away in quick, deceptive zig-zags, now up, now down, right and left, successfully avoiding those murderous bursts from which hurtles the quick death.

As suddenly as it commenced the devil's storm ceases, and no sooner can the pilot breathe than he realises the purpose of his heavy shelling, for the enemy machine has crept close behind him, and the Hun pilot is preparing to loose a leaden stream from his machine gun.

Luckily the pilot has the advantage of speed, and like a flash he dives, turns on his course like lightning and doubles back on to his enemy. As he does so the "*tr-r-r-r-t*" of a machine-gun reaches his ears, and a few holes appear in his plane. That is all the damage the enemy will do. He is slow and heavy, and at the mercy of the faster machine. As the pilot manoeuvres into the position from which he can best destroy his enemy, something causes him to look up, and he realises the reason of his attack by the slow machine and the shower from "Archie" to cover its approach. It is merely the bait to attract his attention whilst the Fokker overhead deals with him.

Quickly he makes up his mind; the slower biplane can wait; he can deal with that after the Fokker. As the monoplane shoots down on him like a rocket-stick he holds on his course till a stream of lead begins to play about him. Then, just as the Fokker is sure of his prey, he banks over to the left, swerves as the baffled machine shoots by, and dives on the enemy like a hawk. The pursuer has now become the pursued, and both machines shoot down almost perpendicularly with awful rapidity. As he dives, the pilot holds back the trigger of his gun and pours a stream of bullets all around his adversary. The latter cannot fire back, his whole safety lies in flight. The dive continues.

As the air rushes about him, singing in the wires of his machine, the pilot places a fresh drum on the barrel of his gun, and again sends messengers of death at his foe. He cannot tell whether he has hit him or not. He must fire until his foe crashes to the earth or all his ammunition is used. The ground is getting rapidly closer. Trees, roads, fields, seem to rush upward towards the pilot, until at last he must try to pull out of his long dive unless he wishes to crash to a thousand pieces on the earth. As he gradually comes into a long smooth glide, he notices the other machine continuing its downward course, and as he sweeps round in a large circle only a few hundred feet from the ground, he sees it crash to earth, the wings collapse and the whole affair become a tangled mass of burning wreckage. Immediately "Archie" commences to burst around him, and he again starts the dance with death.

Meanwhile the other machine, having seen the fate which has overtaken its companion, has fled for home and safety, and the pilot as he climbs and dodges the bursting "Archies," sets his nose towards his first opponent. His machine is small and fast, the Hun is old and slow, and gradually it is overhauled. The pilot's mouth sets in a grim smile as he thinks how he will now proceed to finish the Hun. Unfortunately for him, the Hun realises that his only safety lies below, and making a speedy dive lands safely in a field out of the pilot's reach before a shot has been fired.

During the chase the pilot has gone a considerable distance from his beat, and his time for patrolling is finished, so he sets his course back to the aerodrome.

As he draws near the line "Archie" opens on him again, and he mechanically dips and swerves, keeping a watchful eye aloft for more Fokkers. Suddenly he becomes tense as he sights a speck in the distance; but as he watches his face relaxes, for he recognises a sister machine to his own that has been sent out to relieve him. He waves a greeting as he passes, glances down at the trenches as he crosses over, thinking what a dog's life it must be to live in mud and water—he has absolutely forgotten that he was in those same trenches less than a year ago—and as his aerodrome appears in sight, he commences to switch the engine on and off, descending in one long glide.

The familiar scene flashes up towards him; he touches earth, switches off, and rumbles over the ground towards the hangars. Waiting mechanics rush out to help the machine in, and the pilot climbs stiffly out of his seat and staggers off to the O.C.'s office. He reports himself, and writes out an account of his patrol; and then at last reels to the mess, divests himself of leather coat and helmet, calls for a drink, and sinks into a chair with the latest copy of *La Vie Parisienne* in his hand.

A British Aeroplane Ablaze after a Duel
with a Giant Biplane

CHAPTER 5

Birds of Prey

"Switch off! Petrol on! Suck in!" The pilot calls out the words, and the waiting mechanic slowly twists the huge four-bladed propeller, sucking the explosive mixture into the cylinders of the engine.

"Contact!"

The mechanic steps back, takes a firm grip of one blade, and with a mighty heave stands clear of the machine. Nothing happens; the pilot calls "Switch off!" and once more the blades are slowly swung until a compression stroke is reached. "Contact!" is called again, and this time with a mighty roar the huge engine proclaims its power. Faster and faster whirls the revolving screw, and louder roars the engine, while the crouching mechanics hold on like grim death, their overalls quivering in the current of air. At last, the engine slows down, the pilot waves his hand, chocks are taken from under the wheels, and the machine rolls slowly forward, swaying slightly from side to side at first, but gradually steadying herself as she gains speed until, almost imperceptibly, the earth is left, and she sails aloft in the element so little known by man.

As the aeroplane gains height, the pilot slowly banks and rudders to the left, and swings round in a wide curve. Beneath him he sees his aerodrome, with the machines waiting to ascend. Each machine has several attendant specks—mechanics who attend to her toilet—which gradually grow smaller as the earth recedes. The aerodrome seems very small, a tiny rectangle surrounded by cultivated fields, and his gaze takes it all in at a glance. One of the other machines, crawls over the ground, and then, by its movements, he knows it is in the air. A glance at his aneroid tells him he has already ascended 5,000 feet, so he heads for the town over which he has orders to meet their machines,

31

to escort them on a bomb raid.

His job is to look after the other heavily loaded bombers, and keep off any marauding Hun who may approach. He glances at his map, and recognises the town he is bound for. Already in the distance other aeroplanes are arriving. By this time, he has reached 10,000 feet—the other machines are circling below him and getting into formation. As he looks, another scout arrives at his own level, his companion escort.

Presently the whole body moves off, keeping admirable formation, whilst, ever watchful, above them circle the two escorts. The pilot glances at his instruments—his engine is running beautifully—smiles to himself as he thinks of the many flights he has made in his old 'bus, and settles down to the day's work. His companion is some half a mile away on his right. He glances aloft for a lurking Fokker, but the cloudless sky gives little chance of concealment for these mist-loving birds. Below him, far, far below, he sees the green fields looking like the patchwork cover to a bed, and in front is the long, dark, jagged line which he knows to be the trenches.

Suddenly, far below, he sees a puff of smoke, followed by the faint bang of "Archie," who has opened earlier than usual. There is little danger to him, he knows, for the shell is evidently intended for one of the raiders. The pilot now looks to himself, fingers his gun, and generally prepares for action, as an enemy plane may appear at any moment. The objective is situated a good half-hour's flight over the lines, but at last it appears in sight without an attack being made. As the pilot watches he sees the raid leader swoop, followed in turn by each machine of the formation.

Puffs of smoke follow as each bomb reaches its mark. Suddenly a huge cloud of smoke and a mighty roar show that the main objective has been hit. The enemy ammunition dump has been exploded, huge stores of shell and high explosive vainly stored in preparation of a coming push, have been expended in a moment, great damage has been done to surrounding buildings, and the enemy's moral has suffered severely.

Their work accomplished, the aeroplanes turn to go. On high the escorting pilot glances around. He expects every moment to see a cloud of enemy fighters appear in the sky, for a large aerodrome is close to the dump, and the approach of the bombing squadron must have been observed. It is not long before he sees two machines climbing steeply on his left. These are followed by a third and fourth, and then by two others. Six fighters to attack the squadron. The pilot,

DIVING ON THE ENEMY

while quite aware that the machines he is escorting are armed, knows that it is the duty of himself and his companion to take on the whole six enemy planes while the squadron escapes across the line.

His companion is already diving at the foe, and he gives a quick look round to see that he is safe from attack from the rear before joining in the fray. He singles out a victim, and manoeuvres to catch him unawares. At a range of about thirty yards, he sends a burst of fire from his gun, and swerves sharply to miss the collision. Again, he wheels, but at the same time notices a second machine coming up from behind.

In an instant he makes up his mind. A second burst of fire at the first machine, and he turns on the second. As he banks, he sees a sheet of flame burst from his late foe, and knows that he has accounted for one of the enemy. A sharp crackle sounds in his ears, and several holes appear in the plane beside him. He pushes the control lever forward, dives sharply, zooms up again, wheels round, and finds his opponent banking steeply to avoid him. He fires a short burst at random, and the Hun puts his nose down and runs for it.

He now has time to glance at his partner, and sees that he is being attacked by three planes. The sixth machine is not there, but he spies it out climbing to attack the more defenceless bombing machines. For a moment he hesitates. Shall he go to the help of his comrade, who is hard pressed, or follow the Hun who is attacking the convoy? Even as he hesitates one of the three planes plunges into a spinning nose dive, and he realises that his partner is well able to look after himself. He turns to the solitary Hun, and makes straight for him. Luckily, he has a fast machine, and rapidly overhauls the enemy plane; but the Hun, realising that discretion is the better part of valour, leaves the convoy and heads for his aerodrome.

He spirals rapidly down as the pilot approaches, and lands just in time to save himself. Now, however, is the pilot's chance to use his bombs. He descends to within a few hundred feet, and, as his erstwhile foe runs to a standstill, drops his first bomb. It explodes some fifty feet away, doing no damage; but as the Hun proceeds to leave his machine the second bomb falls, and he and his aeroplane become a tangled mass of wreckage.

Our pilot flies off, zigzagging over the sky amidst a storm of machine-gun fire, unscathed, except for a few holes in his plane. His ammunition is nearly all spent, his convoy is out of sight and he heads for home and his aerodrome. He is no longer anxious to meet a Hun; his chief desire now is for rest and a long drink, for air-fighting is nerve-racking and thirst-causing.

As he approaches the lines, luckily without meeting any Huns, "Archie" begins to play again and he commences the zigzag-dive-zoom in his effort for safety. But either he is overtired, or his luck is out. Closer and closer approach those devilish bursts, until suddenly—a cloud of smoke, a deafening report, and the long swish of rushing air.

How long he remains semi-conscious it is hard to say—probably only a minute or so, for the rush of air quickly revives him. Instinctively he pulls his machine out of the nose dive and looks around. A jagged rent has appeared in his starboard lower plane, through which sticks a broken rib. Several wires are flapping loose, and he is aware of a sharp throbbing in his leg. As he tries to rudder, he finds the limb useless, and it dawns on him that the bone is broken. All this time the bursts have ceased, but as the machine steadies herself and flies again on an even keel, the sky once more becomes covered with puffs of smoke.

Wearily he strives to dodge and twist, but the pain in his leg increases. At last, beneath him he sees the jagged lines of trenches, the "Archies" gradually grow less, and finally he recognises his aerodrome. He pulls himself together for a last effort, and slowly descends. The earth rushes up to meet him, and with the precision of long practice he flattens out and switches off. As the machine bumps over the ground, he is aware of mechanics running out to meet him; he sees a familiar face look over the nacelle, and as he faintly tries to smile, glides off into pleasant unconsciousness, knowing that he has done his work, and will receive a well-earned rest.

CHAPTER 6

The Patrol

Every Wing sends out patrols with great frequency, and it is these patrols which have largely been responsible for the great ascendancy our air service has gained over that of the enemy. The Boche seems to prefer to stay behind his lines, hidden thousands of feet up in the clouds, and wait until he sees his chance of attacking a machine with no danger to himself. Then one long dive on his foe, firing with his machine-gun as he gets within range, and he is off straight down thousands of feet below the British machine.

If his one dive is successful, as it frequently was before we discovered his tricks, all is well; if not, he knows that he would stand little chance against one of the Allies and so makes for home and safety. "*He who fights and runs away may live to fight another day*" is evidently the motto of the Boche. Naturally there are exceptions, and some of the enemy airmen put up excellent fights, and are very good sportsmen, but their general method of attack is one hawk-like dive and then, away.

An instance of the opposite occurred when a British machine— a single-seater—attacked a German scout. They were very equally matched, and for some time manoeuvred round each other firing when good openings occurred. At last, when both machines were riddled with bullets but neither of the pilots nor any vital parts of their aeroplanes had been hit, ammunition gave out on both sides. For a few minutes each circled round, glaring at the other and wondering what would happen next, until each realised that the other was in the same predicament as himself. Thereupon they flew along for some distance smiling amiably, and finally waving *adieu*, each turned for his own aerodrome.

Orders may be given to patrol a certain line, or to circle about in a neighbourhood known to be infested by the enemy. As soon as a hostile machine is sighted chase is given, and the aeroplane is engaged if possible. It is during these aerial combats that the uses of trick flying become apparent, for the pilot who can outmanoeuvre his opponent is the one who will win. Nearly all machines have a blind spot—that is, a certain direction in which they are unable to fire—and it is the object of the attacking pilot to get into this position where he is immune from enemy fire, and then to rake the other machine at leisure. Naturally, each aeroplane turns and twists to avoid letting the other have this advantage, and it needs an exceedingly clever pilot to attain and keep his position while the observer uses the machine-gun.

The sensation during a fight in the air is one of exhilaration and complete confidence in the result. Morale is of a great deal more importance thousands of feet above the earth than actually on it, and it is the superior morale of our Air Service that continually gives us the victory. As an example of that superior morale, take the following affair—an almost incredible piece of bravery that would have been impossible but for the perfect confidence our pilots have in themselves and each other.

Lieut. R——, on F.E. machine, did not return. Believed shot down by Fokker.

This brief official report was sent in by one of our squadrons in France, and concealed a most ghastly tragedy—a possible fate in store for any of our aviators every time they cross the lines. The machine in question had proceeded with others on a bomb raid. It had dropped its bombs on the objective, and was duly returning home a little out of its proper place in the formation—for machines on raids usually fly in formation—and lagging behind the others. Suddenly out of the clouds above dropped a Fokker. Before Lieut. R—— had time to manoeuvre to avoid his opponent, a stream of bullets poured in upon him. Neither he nor his observer was hit, but a shot pierced the petrol tank, and, some nine thousand feet above the earth, the machine became a blazing wreck.

What happened afterwards was reported by the men of an anti-aircraft battery who had witnessed the whole affair. After some minutes, during which the burning aeroplane slowly glided downwards under perfect control, one passenger, seemingly the observer, jumped overboard, evidently preferring the quick death to the slow torture of burning. The pilot, however, like the captain of a ship, though he must have known that his task was hopeless, stuck to his machine to the last, gradually steering it down to earth and safety. Before he could accomplish a quarter of his object the flames did their work; the floor of the nacelle was burnt out, and the blazing body of the pilot dropped through the bottom of the fuselage. The aeroplane crashed in our lines.

Now the sequel to this fearful death—the worst and most dreaded danger the R.F.C. have to face. The hostile pilot who had brought down the machine was well known. Lieut. R—— was not his first victim, and his method of attack was always the same, the only way possible to a Fokker. He hid in the clouds awaiting his opportunity every evening at dusk, and often pounced on a lonely machine—preferably one that had been winged by the German "Archies," but a scheme was arranged to catch him.

Next day, about the same hour of the evening, three British fighting aeroplanes set out on patrol. Capt. D—— flying comparatively low, about 8,000 feet over the lines, while Capt. L—— and 2nd Lieut. W—— flew at about twice the height, concealed in the clouds some little distance off, but keeping a watchful eye on Capt. D——. It was not long before a Fokker Appeared. It hovered about at about 2,000 feet over Capt. D——, but did not venture to attack. All this time Capt. D—— was being heavily shelled. It was part of the scheme for him actually to encourage gunfire and chance being hit. Every time he turned towards the Fokker the latter sheered off; wounded birds were his prey, not hawks with plenty of fight in them.

At last, the shelling got closer and closer to Capt. D——, and suddenly he pretended to be badly hit, stalled his machine, and commenced going down in circles, side-slipping and stalling from time to time. This had the desired effect, and down shot the Fokker to his foe. When he was about 500 feet above Capt. D——, the latter switched on his engine and started fighting the Fokker, who had to pull out of his headlong dive before engaging the British machine. While the Fokker was thus engaged, Capt. L—— and 2nd Lieut. W——, who had watched everything, dived on him from above.

The Fokker saw them, and realised the trap laid for him. All three pilots poured in streams of bullets, 2nd Lieut. W—— firing a drum from 30 yards' range, and Capt. L——, who was above, pumping in a drum and a half from 50 yards. The Fokker nose-dived vertically through the clouds, and crashed in the German lines. Lieut. R——

and his observer were avenged.

But imagine the cool impudence of Capt. D—— waiting over the enemy guns, heavily shelled all the while by the anti-aircraft batteries, and giving the Fokker every chance to attack the target he loved. Imagine at last the long steep dive of the Fokker to his seemingly wounded prey, his realisation, too late, of the trap he was caught in, his attempted escape from the overwhelming odds, and finally the long, sickening dive to earth of the uncontrolled machine, carrying its dead pilot to a second death.

This is war as it is waged in the air; immunity from death may seem to be the luck of a pilot; he may shoot down many machines and be feared far and wide, but if he perseveres death overtakes him sooner or later; and all our pilots know this, and, knowing it, bravely face death a dozen times a day, not caring for themselves, but hoping that when it does come it will be quick—a bullet in the brain—and that they will be spared the sickening dive of the mortally stricken machine or the terrible torture of the flames.

One of the greatest of all the enemy pilots a man who has made his name known all over the earth by his successes in aerial fighting, and who, despite his many victims, was admired and respected by all the R.F.C., met his death at the last at the hands of the veriest novice in the game of war. Immelmann was not only a great fighter, but a real sportsman, and all of our men who had the misfortune to be shot down and captured by him, speak of him as one who was characterised by the lack of those traits which we have come to regard as so typically German. This is the official account of the fight which ended the career of Immelmann:

At about 9 p.m., whilst on patrol duty over Loos, three Fokkers were seen behind the lines. Lieut. McC—— (on an F.E. machine) proceeded over the lines towards them. One Fokker dived away from the other two and left them. The remaining two made for Lens towards another F.E. Lieut. McC—— followed them. Whilst one of them was attacking the F.E. piloted by Lieut. S—— (both machines diving steeply), Lieut. McC—— dived towards the attacking machine and fired upon it. Immediately the Fokker turned to the right from the other F.E., and dived perpendicularly towards the ground. It was seen to crash by No.—— Anti-Aircraft Battery.

Short and concise, shorn of the excitement of the action, is this account of the death of one of the greatest Germans, the victor of countless combats, at the hands of an English novice who had been less than two weeks in France. Imagine the fight in the twilight—it occurred after 9 p.m.—the hawk-like dive of the Fokker on to its prey the dash of the other 'plane to rescue its companion, the spurt of flame from the machine-gun, and the long dive of the uncontrolled Fokker to the earth thousands of feet beneath.

A British officer flew over the lines carrying a wreath from the officers of the squadron in honour of their dead foe. The messenger reached the spot where the interment was to take place as the funeral procession was on its way, and, circling above them, he descended and dropped the wreath as near the grave as possible. Our enemies, in return, a few days later dropped a message bag in our lines expressing their appreciation of our action.

This dropping of message bags is quite a common occurrence, for often when either side brings down a machine, they let the enemy know the fate of the pilot and observer, the extent of their injuries, or sometimes even the address where they are imprisoned. The extent to which these courtesies are carried out varies a great deal according to the locality and the squadrons working on that front.

Naturally machines engaged in patrol work, flying, as they usually are, up and down the enemy side of the line, or round one district especially favoured by the enemy, come in for some heavy shelling.

On several occasions, machines have been shot down with a direct hit, which, needless to say, has blown 'plane, pilot and observer to pieces in mid-air. The effect of bursting shrapnel on an aeroplane, when it does no direct damage, is to cause a violent upsetting of its equilibrium, the degree of course varying with the nearness of the explosion. A close burst may cause the machine to nose-dive, stall, or side-slip, the exact result depending on the part of the machine most in line with the aerial disturbance.

Two officers have a very interesting memento of one heavily shelled patrol which they undertook. They were flying at a very great height—height is essential when combating the Fokker—and the enemy's shells were consistently bursting under them. Suddenly, to the extreme surprise and alarm of the occupants of the aeroplane, a shell fell actually in the nacelle beside the pilot. It fell with no force; just dropped in and lay at the bottom of the machine without exploding. Evidently it had been a well-aimed shell which had reached its extreme range without exploding and was just falling back to earth.

Both pilot and observer claimed it, but as neither, rather naturally, would give in to the other, the "Archie" was cut in half longitudinally, and each man now owns his share—a memory both of an exceedingly curious occurrence and a very lucky escape from a sudden death.

DOGFIGHT IN THE CLOUDS

CHAPTER 7

Headquarters

"Headquarters" is a fairly large *château*, just out of reach of the enemy long-range guns, and is situated in a tiny village some eight kilometres from the nearest town—small, possessed of a cathedral and a town drain, the latter very much in evidence. It also owns a small shop in the cobbled square, close beside the aforesaid town drain, where copies of British periodicals may be obtained about a week after publication at a charge approximating to three times that asked in England.

The owner of the *château*, being a man of means and owning another residence elsewhere, obligingly turned out and left the place in full possession of Headquarters, so that the men have little cause to grumble at their billets. All have a sound roof to sleep under, the clerks have excellent offices, and the officers an excellent mess, for though they are few, passing generals and "brass hats" sometimes condescend to pause and sample the food of the Wing Headquarters.

In addition to a sound roof, the *château* has beautiful grounds—a good lawn on which to partake of afternoon tea, a fine badminton court on which strenuous games are daily waged, to the accompaniment of five-*franc* notes, and last, but by no means least, a most excellent walled garden, on the sunny bricks of which at the proper time glow rosy peaches and juicy pears.

For the rest the garden grows things of practical value—things which have gained fame for the mess all over that particular part of France—grown from seed sent from England, and cultivated under the superintendence of the Equipment Officer, who, besides knowing all about engines and such things, is an enthusiastic gardener. It is for the sake of these fresh green cabbages, these succulent lettuce, and most of all the warm red peaches, that the passing cars so often pause beneath the red-and-blue light that overhangs the gate.

The men for their part have a separate badminton court, and a cricket pitch of sorts in the orchard. That cricket pitch! Taken in combination with the demon bowler it is the most dangerous spot in France. Even the bravest, whose chest is one blaze of many colours gained in the last two years, has been known to flinch, and finally retreat from the wicket after a single over.

There is one thing of importance left unsaid; the *château* owns a billiard table—a table old and worn with the wear of many years, a battered veteran deserving respect and to be left in peace, but nevertheless a billiard table. What if three parts of the cloth are gone, what if the slate seems to have been used for a machine-gun target, what if the solitary cue is tipless, the rest a mere handle without the end, and the balls missing, it still remains a billiard table and a link with respectability and civilisation, which places that headquarters miles above all others.

As to the officers themselves—the Wing Commander is a man young in years, but an officer who joined the Corps on formation. He has a passion for bomb raids, bridge and badminton, thinks his Wing the best in France, and rides straight. I think I am right in saying that his Wing has won more distinctions than any other wing in France—the V.C., several D.S.O.'s and M.C.'s galore having fallen to officers of his squadrons, in addition to many foreign decorations, including the *Médaille Militaire*, the Order of St. Anne, and the Order of St. Stanislaus. Moreover, Immelmann fell to a pilot of this wing.

The Equipment Officer, also a member of the Corps from the beginning, who has risen to his present position from the ranks, is, as already stated, first and foremost a gardener. He has a passion for peaches, pears and parsley, and an intense hatred of caterpillars and slugs. His favourite method of awarding punishment is to give a man fatigue, and send him to pick caterpillars from the cabbages. Apart from his agricultural propensities, he runs the mess, being a marvel in this respect also. He also runs round to squadrons inspecting their transport and aeroplanes, and can instantly produce a new car or a second-hand compass from nowhere.

The adjutant is an unfortunate being who reads endless uninteresting correspondence, censors countless illegible and lengthy letters, makes out orders which are always contradicted later, and generally makes a nuisance of himself, and is frequently told so. He sits by the

THE R.F.C. AT WORK
Aerial action at an altitude of two and a quarter miles
between four British machines and nine German

CHAPTER 8

Artillery Observation

If one branch of the army has benefited more than another by the introduction of aircraft into the art of war, that branch is the Artillery. The gunners would be the last to deny that their tremendous success in the present war is in a large measure due to the machines and men of the R.F.C., who may in truth be called the eyes of the guns.

Batteries are ranged on to targets many miles off and completely invisible to the gunners themselves; hostile batteries, cunningly concealed, are picked out from the air and an inferno of shell directed on to them, effectually silencing them and relieving the bombardment of the trenches; guns are directed on to targets which suddenly present themselves, invisible, except from the air—large bodies of troops in the open, convoys of stores and ammunition, trains disgorging men at a station, all these are dealt with by means of an emergency call from the air which directs every battery in the neighbourhood to fire on the target. All this was impossible before the advent of the aeroplane, and in praising the accuracy and marvellous shooting of the artillery, the work of the Corps which makes these marvels possible should not be forgotten.

Observation machines carry both pilots and observers, and are all fitted with wireless; but on many occasions the pilot alone directs the operations and signals the results of the shots to the batteries for whom he is observing.

Before setting out for an artillery observation flight, the officer who conducts it usually has an interview with the O.C. of the batteries for whom he is working, and arranges any little details of signalling which will simplify the work. He then returns to his aerodrome, gets his altitude, and proceeds to the scene of action, where he identifies his target, and, flying in a figure of eight between target and battery, sends out a call to say that he is ready—that is if the exact position of the target is known to the artillery. He then directs them to send a few sighting shots, and signals the position of the bursts in relation to the target.

At last, when the firing is to his satisfaction, or a direct hit has been obtained, he signals for battery fire on the objective. When the target has been dealt with to his satisfaction, he directs the guns to train on target number two, and so on, until all his targets have been satisfactorily dealt with, when he returns to his station.

Needless to say, the enemy is constantly on the lookout for machine observing for artillery, and the lot of the unprotected pilot is no enviable one. Not only must he keep in the same neighbourhood, undisturbed by "Archies" however close they may burst, but he must, whilst manoeuvring to avoid them, keep a constant eye on the battery in case they signal to him, and watch carefully to see how close the shells burst to the target. Generally, a pilot-observer watches for the flash of his own guns fed then transfers his gaze to the target in anticipation of the bursting shell. He has also to control his machine.

If in addition to this he is suddenly attacked by an enemy aeroplane his position is not to be envied. In the early days of the war, when the pilot was often alone, observation had perforce to be dropped whilst the hostile machine was dealt with; but nowadays, with both pilot and observer in a machine, observation often actually continues whilst a fight is also in progress. In the event of an escort being provided, the fighting machine naturally deals with any Huns who approach in the hope of stopping operations.

Sometimes an extraordinarily good and fleeting target presents itself to the view of the observer in the air. It may be of any nature, but should it be of sufficient importance all other work is dropped for the time, and an emergency call is at once sent out, followed by the exact position of the target on the map used by the artillery. Some at least of the resultant shots are bound to achieve their object, and great damage is often done in this way.

Imagine a machine many thousands of feet in the air engaged on ranging a battery of guns on to a gun emplacement of the enemy. From their elevation pilot and observer can see for many miles, and among the places within observation is the station at W. The attention of the pilot, who is not so closely engaged as the observer, is attracted to the station by the approach of several trains one after the other, and the large number of transport wagons waiting in the yard. He edges a little closer in order to get a better view, and sees that the trains, now at a standstill, are disgorging thousands of troops, who as fast as they leave the railway are hurried into the waiting wagons.

Assured of the importance of what he sees, he draws the attention of the observer to the spot. That worthy seizes the situation at once, refers to his map for the exact position of the station, sends out the emergency call and map reference, and stands by to await results. Both the pilot and the observer impatiently watch the target. The troops are being hurried off faster and faster and faster—already some hundreds are gone. Suddenly, right over the station bursts a shell. It is quickly followed by others, and still more. Shells of every calibre pour into the station, and the surrounding country is covered by a huge pall of smoke.

Gradually the bombardment ceases, and the smoke slowly clears away. The station is demolished, the trains are wrecked, many of the transport wagons are smashed to pieces, and all around lie bodies of countless dead and dying men. The emergency call has achieved its object. In addition to the damage done, a hardly pressed portion of German trench has been robbed of its relief, and must inevitably fall. The pilot and his observer regain connection with their battery and carry on with the work in hand. This is a typical incident in the work of an artillery patrol.

In connection with artillery observation, the work of the Kite-Balloon Sections must not be forgotten. These sections are used solely for observation purposes, and have done much good work in ranging batteries on to the enemy.

Commonly known as "sausages," the balloons consist of a sausage-shaped body with a blob on one end, to which is attached the car containing the observer. The observer carries with him a telephone, the connection of which runs down the cable holding in the balloon. Observation posts are established behind the lines, and from one of these positions the "sausage" ascends, carrying with it an officer observer.

When sufficient altitude has been gained, no more cable is paid out and observation goes on in a similar manner to that employed with aeroplanes. It is not commonly known that the queer shape of these balloons was designed in order to overcome the spinning motion which takes place in an ordinary spherical captive balloon, and which, as well as making observation difficult or impossible, causes the observer to suffer from severe "sea sickness." Occasionally the balloon has its stabilising part shot away, and though it would still remain in the air, the passenger must signal to be hauled down as the spinning soon commences.

In the case of attack by ordinary shell fire the officer remains at his post as long as possible, only allowing himself to be hauled down if the fire is extremely accurate and the whole affair is in danger of being shot away. Should the connecting cable be severed and the wind blow the balloon in the direction of the enemy, the occupant must make use of his parachute and jump overboard, hoping to land our side of the line.

Occasionally this last resort does not act, the parachute failing to open, but generally speaking the passenger safely reaches earth with little violence. It is computed that the force of the fall is only equal to that of an ordinary drop of six feet, and certainly a large number of lives have been saved in this way.

The officers and men of the K.-B.S. are specially trained for the work, though many before entering this section of the R.F.C. graduate as flying officers, and fly in aeroplanes for some months. Should an accident or other reason cause them to lose their nerve and become dangerous as aeroplane pilots, they often transfer to the K.-B.S., where there is no delicate machine to manage, though some of the delights of the air still remain.

It is rarely that a German aeroplane attacks one of our observation kite-balloons. When a "sausage" *is* attacked by aircraft, the general method is to pour in bullets with the hope of hitting the observer, or making things so warm for him that the balloon must be hauled down. When the thing is on the ground, and so presents a firmer target, bombs are dropped in the hope of entirely destroying it. When incendiary bullets are used the envelope may be pierced and the gases ignited, causing everything to become a blazing wreck.

Though the Germans do not often attack our kite-balloons, the pilots of the R.F.C. on many occasions have brought down those of the enemy by direct attack. One of the best examples of this occurred when Lieut. N—— destroyed three Boche balloons on one afternoon. He charged the first at its own elevation of a few thousand feet, pumping in incendiary bullets as he got within range. When it seemed that he must inevitably collide with the "sausage" he "zoomed" the machine, shooting up into the air and over the enemy.

As he passed over the top be dropped an incendiary bomb which caused the gases to ignite, and the balloon fell in flames to the ground.

The second balloon he charged in a similar manner, but the bullets alone caused it to fall in flames. As he charged the third target, the observer, probably having seen the fate of the two others, caused himself to be hauled down before he could be damaged. Lieut. N———, however, descended to within a few hundred feet of the ground, and despite heavy fire dropped two bombs, the second of which achieved its object and set the balloon alight.

Perhaps the work of the Kite-Balloon Section is a trifle less showy than that of other departments of the R.F.C. but it is none the less useful, and it is easy to realise that a fixed object, flying at a height of only a few thousand feet, is a much better target for Fritz when he feels nasty than a fast flying aeroplane at an altitude which makes it appear a speck in the sky.

So much for artillery observation.

CHAPTER 9

Against the Odds

As he leaves his quarters for the aerodrome the pilot shivers. It is less the coolness of the early morning air than the foreboding of ill, the sense of impending disaster that comes at times to all airmen. He had flown late the night before, had not reached his aerodrome until after dark, and had endured a severe strafe by "Archie"; that is, the strafe was more severe even than usual which says a lot. Now as he watches his machine being wheeled out from the hangar, he wonders what the day will bring forth and he shivers again.

Being a scout pilot, he has no observer to trouble about, so soon climbs into his place and has the engine humming. He tests his gun mountings, feels the controls, and at last gives the signal to his waiting mechanics.

The tiny pusher rushes over the ground for a short space, and then literally bounds into the air in obedience to the pilot's touch. He is on the early morning patrol, and the sooner he is relieved the better he will be pleased.

In the greyness of the early morning, fields and roads loom faint and indistinct below him as he makes his way in the direction of the trenches. At last, he sees the ugly ragged scars which mark the uttermost limit of comparative safety and his post is reached. He crosses into enemy territory and wheels parallel to the line. For the next two hours, until his relief arrives, he will fly up and down a given stretch of front on the lookout for anything that may arrive, and the target of every "Archie" within range.

Suddenly a faint "*Bang! bang! Bang!*" causes him to look down, and he sees the morning performance begin. Three tiny puffs of cotton-wool-like smoke appear below him and the machine shivers slightly.

The range is bad and he pays no regard to the bursting death. Another cloud appears, this time above him, and others in front, behind, and on either side. Each burst is closer to him than the last, and he prepares to manoeuvre.

A burst almost under his nose violently rocks the whole machine; "*zip!*" goes a bullet through the fabric, and a tiny hole appears in the plane. "Archie" has found the range, and it is advisable to dodge. He puts down the nose of his aeroplane and drops a couple of hundred feet, zigzagging rapidly the while. When the range is again found he zooms his machine and carries on until he is at last out of range of the battery. He has a few minutes' peace before the next battery picks him up, and the performance is repeated until he reaches the limit of his patrol and turns to retrace his course.

Suddenly, in the midst of a prolonged and heavy strafe, "Archie" ceases fire, and in the sudden calm, undisturbed save for the unnoticed roar of his engine, the pilot has time to look about him. As he does so he shivers again—ever so slightly, it is true—a shiver hardly of cold so much as of a black foreboding. He looks up to see the evil shape of a Fokker overhead, and as he looks, she dives and a stream of bullets plays about him.

Fokkers, however, are of no importance if properly handled, and the pilot avoids the plunging fire of the Hun as he rushes past, and dives after him, pouring a leaden stream from his gun. Apparently, he has no luck, for the monoplane flattens out many hundred feet below and retires in the direction of the Hun aerodrome. "Archie" bursts out again, and the air is dotted with puffs of whistling death as the scout climbs again into the blue of the morning air.

The pilot glances at his watch; half his time is over, and he begins to feel cheerier. "Archie" has slackened off again, and there are no signs of waiting Huns in the surrounding sky. He looks down at the earth 10,000 feet below, all torn and jagged in the morning sunlight, with patchy of brilliant green away from the trenches. Puffs of smoke arise all along the line, and in his imagination, he can hear the roar of the morning strafe. An immense cloud of smoke arises, and he recognises the firing of a mine. As the strafe clears off, he can discern the point between the trenches, and realises that a life and death struggle is being fought for its possession. It is not so many months since he took part in a similar affair. He was a "gravel-crusher" then.

He wakens out of his reverie and looks around. In the distance are two machines—scouts of a similar type to his own. They are circling round some miles behind our lines, apparently waiting to convoy a bomb raid. One by one the bombers appear, gain their formation, and the whole body sweeps over the lines a thousand feet or so below the patrolling scout. He watches them until they vanish from right. Every available battery seems trained on the raiders, and he continues in peace.

A few minutes later three black specks appear on the horizon and rapidly grow larger, until he recognises the latest type of enemy fighter. Seemingly they have come with the intention of catching the raiders, but have arrived too late. The pilot knows this and realises that he will now become the object of their attack. He glances at his watch again. In half an hour his relief will arrive. If only he can hold out till then! Half an hour is a long time in the air. Ten minutes usually suffice to decide a combat. He realises his only chance, jams on a drum of ammunition and charges straight at the nearest Hun.

The three machines separate, but he sticks to his prey and reserves his fire. There is no time to manoeuvre. His enemy opens fire at 100 yards—a wandering fire that does no harm—but the pilot holds his peace. Gone are all his forebodings; his one desire is to see that malignant black-crowed machine burst into flames. At thirty yards he presses the trigger and a stream of lead and flame pours from his gun. So close is he that he can see the enemy observer drop forward in his seat as he zooms the machine clear of the impending collision. He banks steeply, turns in a second and empties half a drum into his foe at close range. The aeroplane bursts into flame, and a thrill of joy runs through the pilot. It is his first victim.

However, he has little time to moralise, for both the other machines charge down on him. Several holes appear in the white spread of his wings and a sting in his chin makes him draw his gauntleted hand across his face. It is only a surface scratch—just enough to draw blood and make him still more anxious to finish off his foes. Drum after drum of ammunition is fired. His planes are speckled with holes, but no vital place has been touched. Despite his superior speed he cannot outmanoeuvre his enemies, for they are two to one and both clever pilots.

With a thrill of horror, he realises that he has placed his last drum of ammunition on the gun. It has not occurred to him to flee, which he could easily do, and he prepares for one last effort before he is helpless. As he swings his machine a stabbing numbness seizes his leg, and the next instant his left arm falls useless. Gritting his teeth, he drops the control and leaves the machine to look to itself. One of his enemies is in the line of fire, and he pours out bullets from his gun.

His wounded leg gives agonies as he forces it against the rudder-bar; blood is streaming down his arm and his head is beginning to swim. He is dimly conscious of his gun jamming; and now it is the end of the last drum, and he sees a machine bearing down upon him as in a final whirl he becomes oblivious to it all.

It is only for a second, however, and his senses return in a dazed way. He is somehow conscious that it is all over, and wonders why they don't finish him off. He plucks up strength and looks up, and—wonder of wonders!—both nightmare shapes are vanishing in the distance. He languidly turns to seek a solution, and sees a twin machine to his own. His relief has arrived, and he is able to go.

Waveringly in intervals of consciousness and oblivion, he returns to his aerodrome. The mechanics realise by the flight that something is wrong and run out to meet the machine. The pilot instinctively flattens out and switches off, and as his "'bus" bumps to a standstill he summons up his failing strength, and murmurs contentedly: "Anyhow, I strafed one of the blighters!"

"Trench Strafing": British low-flying scouts co-operating in an infantry attack on the Western Front

Chapter 10

Bombing and Photography

> The following bombing will be carried out by No.— Squadron at night (10 p.m., 12 midnight, and 2 a.m.). At each of these times three machines will bomb respectively P———, C———, H———.

Thus, the Operation Orders one evening in France. Quite ordinary orders too, for bombing is carried out day and night incessantly—by day with the object of damaging material, by night chiefly to annoy the Hun and have a bad effect on his morale. Bombing by night is usually carried out on towns and villages known to be resting-places of the German troops, and it is part of the work of the R.F.C. to see that the Hun never rests.

Fritz after a hard spell in the trenches is withdrawn to some shell-torn village behind his lines to rest. He enters the ruined house that forms his billet, and with a sigh of contentment at reaching such luxury after the miseries of trench life prepares to sleep in peace—a peace undisturbed by raiding Britons or well-placed mines. He dreams of home, fair-haired buxom damsels, *würst* and *sauerkraut*, and then out of the night comes the terror of the air. A bomb falls in his billet, exploding with a terrific report, and doing damage to the already mined walls.

Possibly a few of his comrades are wounded or killed. Other explosions take place close by, and the whole village becomes a mass of roaring Germans. Then the explosions cease, the noise of engines grows fainter, and all becomes quiet, but Fritz does not sleep again. His nerves are jangled, all possibility of sleep is gone, and he momentarily expects to hear more explosions, heralding the arrival of yet another bombing squadron. Next day he is in a worse condition than after a night in the trenches, and this continues night after night until the period of "rest" is over and he returns to the expected turmoil of the trenches. But it is the unexpected which harms, the constant fear of death from the sky which disturbs Fritz's peace of mind and causes him to curse our Flying Corps and all who are concerned with it.

These night raids do little damage to material except by chance—in this they are comparable to the Zeppelin raids on England—but the damage to German morale is enormous; the days bring much labour, and the night does not bring the expected rest; nerves are constantly on the alert listening for the approach of hostile aircraft which hurl death from above, and "rest" is a period of anxious moments which tire more than the firing of the trenches. No wonder night raids are carried out so constantly. No wonder the Hun coins such choice epithets to hurl at the Corps.

From the aerial point of view things are different. A pilot warned for night flying takes it as he takes everything else—with apparent unconcern—It's all in the day's work. He realises that he will have an uninteresting ride in the dark; the danger from "Archie" will be small—an aeroplane is a difficult target to keep under observation with a searchlight—and the danger from hostile aircraft will be smaller still.

He realises that he will have to find his target in the dark, and that if his engine fails it will be rough luck. He may also lose his way and have to descend at another aerodrome. In that case he will remain until daylight, and then rejoin his squadron. The whole journey from start to finish will be more or less devoid of interest—no "Archies" to dodge, no Huns to fight, and no possibility of observing much of what damage is done by his bombs.

He leaves the aerodrome and quickly climbs up into the darkness. Below him are the very faint outlines of fields, woods, and villages. Ponds and streams show more distinctly, and the roads show faintly through the night. When he has attained sufficient height, at a signal from the leader he heads for the lines. Over the trenches the star shells of the infantry may be seen, occasionally the flash of a badly concealed gun glints in the darkness, or the exploding bombs of a trench raiding party cause tiny sparks to glimmer far below.

Probably the enemy, hearing the sound of engines, will turn on his searchlights and sweep the sky with long pencils of light. The pilot may be picked up for a second, and a trifle later the angry "*Bang, bang, bang*" of "Archie" may be heard, firing excitedly at the place where the aeroplane ought to be but is not; the pilot has probably dipped and changed his course since he was in the rays of the searchlight. He may be caught again for an instant, and the performance is repeated.

Before long the vicinity of the target is reached, and he prepares to drop his bombs. A little before he is over the spot the first bombs will be released, for the trajectory of the bomb follows the course of the machine if the latter keeps on a straight course, and when it explodes the aeroplane is still overhead. Down far below will be seen a tiny burst of flame; possibly a large fire blazes up, and the pilot knows that his work is good. He then turns and repeats his performance until all his bombs are exhausted, when he turns for home. Bombs are usually dropped from a low altitude at night in order to be surer of hitting the target.

During the performance any local searchlights are turned on, "Archie" gets busy, and a merry game of hide-and-seek in and out the beams takes place. If the aeroplane is very low—and bombs are sometimes dropped from a height of only a few hundred feet—it is highly probably that the bursting shells do more damage than the aeroplane's bombs, and it is almost impossible to wing an aeroplane by night.

Over the lines the pilot probably meets more searchlights, dodges them, and gradually descends. Below him he sees the aerodromes of the surrounding squadrons lighted up for landing purposes. He then lands, hands his machine over to the mechanics and turns in.

So much for night bombing. By day it is different. Though at night it is billets which usually form the target with the object of destroying German morale, by day bombing is carried out for the purpose of damaging specific objects, and occasionally they are damaged pretty severely. Railroads, dumps of stores and ammunition and enemy aerodromes are the favourite targets. The raiding machines fly in formation, and are surrounded by other machines used solely for protective purposes.

All the 'planes meet at a prearranged rendezvous well our side of the line at a certain time and a given altitude. A Flight Commander leads the raid, and when he sees that all machines are in their correct positions, he fires a signal light, and the whole move off to their objective. Needless to say, such a cloud of aeroplanes presents a tempting target to "Archie," and shells burst all around the raiders.

The bombing machines may carry any number of bombs.

Although the escorting fighters are primarily for protective purposes, they usually carry two or three bombs to use if necessary. Once over the target the fighters scatter and patrol the neighbourhood, while the bombers discharge their missiles on the objective. Usually, unless anti-aircraft fire is very heavy, they descend a few thousand feet to make surer of the target, and when their work is completed rise again to the level of the escort.

Results can usually be fairly judged by day—an ammunition dump, needless to say, quickly shows if it is hit, and stores soon burst into flame. Railway stations or junctions show clearly injury to buildings or overturned trucks, but the damage to the track itself is hard to estimate. Aerodromes may be bombed for the purpose of destroying enemy machines in their hangars, or merely in order to spoil the landing by blowing holes all over the surface.

It is with great delight that a pilot remarks in his report that a hostile aeroplane surrounded by mechanics was about to ascend, but that instead he had descended to within a few hundred feet and obtained a direct hit, with the result that the enemy machine—including the surrounding men—"seemed to be severely damaged."

One officer on a bomb raid saw his chance in this way, descended to 400 feet under intense rifle fire, successfully bombed the enemy machine which was just emerging from its hangar, and then tried to make off. Unfortunately, at this moment his engine petered out, possibly on account of the enemy's fire, and he had to descend. By skilful planing he managed to land about three-quarters of a mile away, in full view of the enemy. Instead of giving up the ghost and at once firing his machine, this officer jumped out and, utterly unperturbed by the German fire or by the Huns making across country to take him prisoner, commenced to inspect the engine.

Luckily, he found the cause of the trouble at once, put it right—it was only a trifling mishap—adjusted the controls and swung the propeller. The engine started, he jumped in with the nearest Hun only a hundred yards off, and opening the throttle raced over the ground and into the air pursued by a futile fusillade of bullets. His engine held out, and he safely regained his aerodrome after having been reported missing by his comrades. For this escapade he received the Military Cross—a well-earned reward.

When all the bombs have been dropped and the formation resumed, the machines head for home. It is on the homeward journey that events may be expected, for time enough has elapsed for the Hun to detail a squadron to intercept our returning aeroplanes and pick off any stragglers that may fall behind.

It is a favourite Boche manoeuvre to detail some of his slow machines to entice our fighters away from the main body, and when this has been accomplished to attack the remainder with Fokkers, which dive from aloft on to the bombing machines. This trick it now well known, and the fighters rarely leave their charges until the latter are in comparative safety.

Sometimes a Hun of more sporting character than his brothers will wait alone for the returning convoy, hiding himself thousands of feet up in the clouds until he sees his moment, and singling out a machine dive at it, pouring out a stream of bullets as he falls. Sometimes he achieves his object, and a British machine falls to earth, but whatever the result the Hun does not alter his tactics. He dives clean through the whole block of machines down many thousands of feet, only flattening out when close to the ground.

The whole affair is so swift—just one lightning dive—that long before a fighter can reach the Hun the latter is away thousands of feet below, and heading for home and safety. Every Fokker pilot knows that once his surprise dive is over, he has no chance against another machine—the build of the Fokker only allows this one method of attack—and he does not stop to argue about it. His offensive dive becomes a defensive one—that is the sole difference.

Sometimes a large squadron of German machines, composed of various types of aeroplanes, intercepts a returning formation. If it attacks a grand aerial battle ensues. The British fighting machines spread out in a screen to allow the bombers a chance to escape, and then attack the Huns as they arrive. In one place one British aeroplane will be defending itself from two or three German machines; close by two or three of our "'buses" will be occupied in sending a Hun to his death; elsewhere more equal combats rage, and the whole sky becomes an aerial battlefield where machines perform marvellous evolutions, putting the best trick flying of pre-war days very much in the shade.

No sooner has a pilot accounted for his foe—either killing him, forcing him to descend, or making him think discretion the better part of valour—than he turns to the help of a hard-pressed brother, surprising the enemy by an attack from the rear or otherwise creating a diversion. A single shot in the petrol tank proves fatal loss of pressure ensues, the engine fails, and the pilot is forced to descend. He can usually land safely, but should he be in enemy territory he must fire his machine and prepare for a holiday in Germany.

Should he be fortunate enough to plane over our lines little damage is done; the tank can be repaired and the aeroplane made serviceable again. But for the time being he is out of the fight. Sometimes the escaping petrol may ignite, and the pilot and observer perish in the flames—the most terrible fate of all.

The aerial battle ends in one of two ways—one side is outmanoeuvred, outnumbered, and has lost several machines and flies to safety, or, the more usual ending, both sides exhaust their ammunition—only a limited quantity perforce being carried—and the fight is of necessity broken off. Meanwhile the bombing machines have probably crossed the line in safety and their duty is finished. Should they be attacked by a stray enemy they are armed and quite capable of guarding themselves against any attack other than one in force.

During these bomb raids photographs of the target are frequently obtained, or should the staff require photographs of any district passed over on the journey they are generally secured by bombing machines. It is wonderful what minute details may be seen in a photograph taken at a height of from eight to twelve thousand feet. The camera is generally attached to the aeroplane, though it may be used by the observer holding it in his hands in a more or less ordinary manner.

In appearance the camera is quite unlike the usual type of lens and bellows arrangement, and greatly resembles the cheap fixed focus enlarger used by some amateurs. It is fitted with a large aperture lens and a roller blind shutter working at fairly fast speeds, though not so fast as would be imagined when considering the speed of the aeroplane from which it is used.

When it is remembered that a single machine crossing the line is heavily shelled it may be conceived what an immense concentration of "Archies" is made on the raiders on their return. It is remarkable what feeble results are obtained considering the intensity of the bombardment, but rarely is a machine brought down though casualties naturally occur occasionally. Sometimes an officer is hit with remarkable results, and at least one pilot had an extraordinarily narrow escape when returning from a raid.

Lieut. C——, in company with other pilots, had successfully bombed his target and meanwhile been heavily shelled, with the result that his engine was not giving its full number of revolutions, and he lagged a little behind the rest of the formation. No hostile aircraft appeared, and all went well until he was about to cross the lines, when a terrific bombardment was opened on him. He dodged and turned to the best of his ability, but a well-aimed shot burst just above him and a piece of an "Archie" shell hit him on the head, not seriously wounding him, but knocking him unconscious.

The machine, deprived of the guiding hand, immediately got into a dive, and commenced a rapid descent from 10,000 feet, carrying the unconscious pilot with it, to be dashed to pieces on the ground. Whether the push of air, the sudden increase of pressure, or the passing off of the effect of the blow caused the disabled man to come to his senses is not known, but when the aeroplane was only a few hundred feet from the ground Lieut. C—— recovered his senses sufficiently to realise his position and managed to pull the machine up and make a landing. He then lapsed into unconsciousness again. Had he remained in his state of collapse half a minute longer he would inevitably have been killed.

Another curious case of wounding was that of Lieut. H——, who was also returning from a bomb raid. When flying through the heavily shelled zone his machine was hit by a shell, which passed through the floor by the pilot's seat and out at the top without exploding. Lieut. H—— thought it must have been very close to his leg, but he was so fully occupied with manoeuvring to dodge other shells that he had no time to think of it. He neared the line and began to plane down, when he was aware of feeling of faintness; but pulling himself together he landed his machine, and attempted to get out.

It was only then that he realised that his leg was shot almost completely off above the knee—the lower leg was merely hanging by a piece of skin. Incredible as it may seem, the shell which hit his machine also tore through the leg—luckily without exploding—unknown to Lieut. H——. Probably the force of the blow and excitement of the moment caused it to pass unnoticed, and the torn nature of the wound helped to close the arteries and prevent his bleeding to death. He recovered and is still engaged in doing his duty for the duration of the war.

THE PHOTOGRAPHIC SECTION, R.F.C.

Few people are devoid of all knowledge of things photographic, but still fewer realise the multiplicity of uses to which the camera may be put and the many ways in which it is employed by the Royal Flying Corps.

Normally the use in war of the camera is for reconnaissance purposes, but though generally considered—by the uninitiated—to be a more or less soft and safe job, aerial photography under war conditions is an exceedingly unpleasant duty to undertake. In the early days when the pilot set out alone with the camera strapped to his machine, and had to patrol backwards and forwards over a certain area making his exposures at exactly the right moment, dodging "Archie" at the same time, and often having a combat with a Hun machine which objected to his presence as an interlude in the operations, the photographic reconnaissance was a thing to be avoided.

Now that more machines are available, the pilot who is doing the reconnaissance is generally provided with an escort whose sole duty is to drive off enemy aeroplanes which attempt to interfere with the operation. Nevertheless, "Archie" continues to strafe merrily, and the photographer has to endure it without any means of retaliation until his job is finished and he is free to return to his aerodrome.

Photographing a town is no easy task, involving as it does many journeys into the air and often the exposure of several hundred plates. Even after the pilot has covered the whole of the requisite ground and obtained all the necessary negatives, there is still an immense amount of work to be done by the photographic section.

Many towns in Egypt have been photographed by this method, and owing to the clearness of the atmosphere the results are of unparalleled excellence, photographs taken from 8,000 feet showing even the tracks of the aeroplanes on the sand of the aerodromes and the very spray of waves breaking on the reefs.

After the war it is certain that the Photographic Section R.F.C. will develop enormously.

A Zeppelin's lurid end above the Clouds

CHAPTER 11

"Per Ardua ad Astra"

"Five o'clock, sir!"

The weary pilot turns in his bed, yawns and inquires about the weather. He mutters a curse when he hears that the weather is good—ideal for instruction, in fact—for he is an instructor pilot of a training squadron, and must needs be up betimes to take advantage of the calm of the early morning. A rough morning means an extra three hours in bed, but in the ideal winter climate of Egypt such mornings are few and far between.

The sky is just flushing with dawn as he turns out and makes his way to the aerodrome. The huge doors are already open and a machine is being wheeled out. A few minutes later the roar of the engine wakes the silence, and a cloud of sand is thrown up by the draught from the propeller. Then the noise ceases and the quiet stillness of the early morning settles again.

By twos and threes sleepy-eyed pupils arrive on the scene, clad in a miscellany of garments, for dress regulations are not too strictly adhered to on early morning flying. Other instructors arrive, fresh machines are brought out, and the whole aerodrome becomes a scene of great activity. Soon a 'plane takes the air to sample the morning, and it is easy to see by the steadiness of its flight that not a current exists in the upper regions.

This is a squadron where a certain number of pupils are already flying solo, and it is during these first solo flights that a beginner's nerve is most tested. On this occasion, however, the instructor wishes to take up a new machine to test before handing it over to one of his pupils to try his skill on. Calling out to one of the waiting pupils to put on helmet and goggles and jump in—for the chance of giving experience in the air is never neglected—the pilot climbs into his seat and soon has the engine giving its preliminary roar. Satisfied that all is well with the engine, he waves the waiting mechanics aside, and the machine glides over the sandy aerodrome, leaving a cloud of sand in its wake. Almost imperceptibly he takes her off the ground and climbs in wide circles. At present he does not indulge in stunts; elevation is necessary for the safe performance of fancy flying.

Below him he sees the aerodrome, distinguishable amidst the surrounding sand by the tracks made by the aeroplane wheels. Machines stand outside the hangars, two crawl over the ground, one about to ascend, the other just having completed a flight. Palm groves dot the country, which is intersected by irrigation canals. Soon the sandy area is left, and below is a vast area of fresh green with myriads of ditches gleaming in the sun. As far as the eye can see this intense green prevails, the green fertile land of the Nile Delta. Everything is flat. Even from the elevation of a few hundred feet no hills or even knolls are visible.

The freshness of the morning air just being warmed by the newly-risen sun intoxicated the pilot, and he rises higher and higher until his aneroid registers 8,000 feet. Here he feels safe, and proceeds to test his machine. First a steeply-banked turn to the left, then to the right. Next, he climbs the aeroplane so steeply that she stalls and drops tail foremost. The passenger turns round with a frightened look in his eyes, but calms own when he receives a smile of assurance from the pilot. The machine recovers herself in a few hundred feet, and the pilot steadies himself for a loop. Before doing so he touches the passenger on the shoulder and signifies his intention, for he is a kindly instructor and does not wish to "put the wind up" the pupil.

Then he pushes the control lever well forward, the machine dives almost vertically, and at the right moment is pulled back and over, and on to an even keel again. The passenger has a momentary view of the whole earth turning a somersault, the engine is first below and then above him, everything reels, and he gives himself up for lost—nothing on earth can prevent an awful crash—and then suddenly realises that it is all over, and he is still alive. The sudden relief causes him to be violently sick, and the pilot decides that it is time to return home.

They reach the aerodrome at a height of several thousand feet, and a steep spiral which again causes the unhappy pupil to give up hope brings them well down. The engine is throttled back, the nose of the plane dips, the earth rushes up and the machine rumbles over

67

Flight Sub-Lieutenant R. A. Warneford, R. N., blows up a
Zeppelin airship between Ghent and Brussels, following which
his aeroplane turned upside down.

the ground to a standstill. Pilot and pupil get out, the latter trying to appear as though he had enjoyed it.

Satisfied that the machine is flying well the instructor picks out a pupil who is well advanced and tells him to make his first solo—a generous order, as a first solo often means at least a crashed undercarriage. The pupil enters the machine, and at last rushes over the sand into the air. He steers a good course round the aerodrome, not climbing on his turns or committing any very glaring faults, and finally throttles back and commences his glide to earth. All goes well until he is within an ace of landing, when he flattens out a trifle too late and bumps up into the air. Luckily, he keeps his head, opens his throttle, and reaches ground safely, though he bumps over the aerodrome like a cat on hot bricks.

"More landings" is the instructor's mental comment, and he proceeds to take up another pupil and give him dual instruction. A heavy-handed one this—one never likely to make a good pilot. By the time the instructor has taken him in hand for ten minutes he has shouted himself hoarse in vain efforts to make his voice heard above the noise of the engine, and saved the pupil from imminent death at least, three times.

So, it continues. In Egypt flying often commences in the early morning and continues throughout the day, with only a rest for a couple of hours at midday when the air becomes too bumpy for instruction.

Long before the end of the day the pilot is getting pale and hollow-eyed with the strain of continuous instructing in the air—sometimes as much as seven hours a day actual flying.

As he stands on the Tarmac outside the hangars in the cool of the evening watching his latest soloist perform, he suddenly stiffens, and his gaze concentrates on the machine in the air. To the casual observer everything is normal, but his trained ear has caught the sound of a failing engine. As he watches, the machine stalls, side slips, half recovers, and turns into a nose dive. She is falling behind the hangars, and as the pilot commences to run, he hears the crash as the machine reaches earth. Calling for the ambulance and shouting for everyone to keep back where they are, he rushes round the shed. A tangled heap of wreckage lies on the sand.

The machine has fallen practically perpendicularly, the planes have folded back, the fuselage has doubled up, ribs peer through the torn fabric, and a tangled mass of iron represents the engine. Standing by and looking very white is the erstwhile pilot. Despite the awful crash he has escaped unhurt, as is often the case. Beyond a shaking he is quite fit, and in a fearful funk as to what his instructor will have to say. The latter is so relieved to find his pupil safe that he relieves his feelings by giving the unfortunate pupil one of the severest jacketings he has ever had. The pupil is duly penitent and very much ashamed of himself; also, he has not the slightest desire ever to fly again—for the time being. Tomorrow he will be as keen as ever.

For the night, however, the instructor decides that enough has been done, and dismisses all his pupils. The day has been an average one. He has done about five hours' flying, has tormented his soul with anxiety for the pupils whose lives are in his hands; he is tired out, and knows that the same performance must be repeated on the morrow.

CHAPTER 12

A Slack Day Overseas

It must not be thought that all days are flying days in France, though indeed it is few on which some sort of aerial work does not take place. A typical "slack day" is not, as many may think, one on which the wind blows strongly and the rain comes down—it needs a very bad wind to prevent some pilots taking the air—but more of the dull, grey, misty type when one cannot see much more than a hundred yards or so through the haze, and the clouds, though not actually pouring their substance on the earth, are only a few hundred feet above the ground.

On these days flying is impossible; the pilot would be quite unable to find his way about, and even should he essay to steer by compass—an almost impossible task to do with sufficient accuracy—he would find himself utterly unable to see anything either on the ground or in the air, the sole object of his flight. On these days, then, work must be done at home, and all machines undergo thorough inspection, adjustments are made, and the pilot has any pet fitting he may fancy attached to his aeroplane.

After a limited number of hours flying the engine is taken out and overhauled—thoroughly taken down, cleaned, new parts fitted and toned up to perfection before being put back. Each wire and cable has a certain life and shows certain signs of decay; at the least symptom of wearing out it must be replaced. Holes appear in the fabric of the wings; these must be patched, or rain will find its way into the interior, rot the fabric, rust the wires, and decay the ribs. The bracing wires which keep planes and fuselage properly adjusted need truing up with great frequency, and the whole dimensions of the aeroplane must be checked as often as possible. After a certain length of time in the air the whole machine—like the engine—must be overhauled. Constant supervision Is requisite in order to get the most out of the aero plane with the greatest safety to pilot and observer, and it is chiefly oh these slack days that the little bits of work that mean so much to all concerned can be done.

Of course, there is another side to the day, and the perfect Squadron Commander who always has his machines in good order thinks of the welfare of his men, and usually organises something which takes the minds of officers and men alike off the monotony of the daily round. Sports may occupy the afternoon, and a concert in the evening will bring visitors from all the surrounding air stations like flies to a honeypot. During the summer there are very few non-flying days, so that naturally football reigns supreme during the slack afternoons on winter days.

Sometimes matches are arranged with neighbouring squadrons if they are close enough to make transport easy, but the general thing is an inter-flight competition, in which each flight plays all the others. Half-hour games are the rule, so that the whole set can be played off in one strenuous afternoon, N.C.O.'s and man entering wholeheartedly with great rivalry into the affair, and the officers backing up their flights and taking it in turns to act as referee. The football is not of a very high order, but plenty of exercise and give and take are indulged in, the minds of all concerned are taken off their work, and, greatest of all, it helps to keep the men fit.

The work of the R.F.C. in France does not call for too much vigorous exercise, and these afternoons are splendid tonics for everyone. In England, especially on aerodromes where training is in progress, the mechanics get plenty of exercise running out to start up the engine of some beginner who in landing has "lost his prop." through misjudgement. All sports, too, are encouraged, especially running and swimming, for men of the R.F.C. do not have the long route marches which help so greatly to keep the infantryman fit.

After football, probably the most popular sporting event is a boxing tournament, and sparring of a very high class frequently takes place in these squadron affairs. A ring is soon fixed up in one of the hangars, or even in the open aerodrome, contests are arranged for the various weights, and with officers to judge, the men are soon going hammer and tongs. Short contests—three rounds of two minutes each—are generally the rule, but there is no dodging about and unnecessary foot work to waste time.

During the whole round both men are hard at it, plenty of give and take, some good boxing, more vigorous hammering for the pure love of the primitive instinct to fight, but no waiting and dodging and other efforts to gain time. The spectators indulge in chaff freely at the expense of the boxers, but it is all good-humoured—as free from animosity as are the blows exchanged in the ring. A Gnome engine cylinder makes an excellent gong, and time is sounded in a manner appropriate to the Corps.

The evening is usually given up to an impromptu concert. Officers from neighbouring squadrons arrive for dinner—for most squadrons run a mess in more or less civilised fashion—and afterwards a hangar or other convenient building is crowded with men, a violin or other instrument appears from somewhere, and the sergeant-major announces that 2nd A.M. R—— will oblige with "The Rosary."

Many papers have given reproductions of weird songs purporting to be composed and used by men of the R.F.C., but, personally, after nearly three years with the Corps, the writer has not heard any of them, though he must say he has seen cuttings from the said papers hung up in billets as curiosities. The old sentimental songs and the latest bits from the revues generally fill the programme, mixed with recitations of the nature of "The Green Eye of the Little Yellow God" and humorous parodies of "Excelsior" and the "Village Blacksmith."

It is rarely that a new song is heard; it would probably be received badly, however good it might really be. Old favourites are best, and if they possess a rollicking chorus, so much the better. Those who have not heard a few hundred healthy men singing the last chorus to "Way Down in Dixie" as an end up to an evening concert have missed much, and should rectify the omission at the earliest opportunity.

Needless to say, "God Save the King" comes at the last, sung in a stately manner very different from that in which the choruses have been rolled out, accompanied by a squeaky violin, a wheezy concertina, and a rather liquid cornet, the whole body of men meanwhile standing as if each individual had swallowed the barrack-room poker.

And so, to bed. Officers reach the mess to have "just one more" before going into the cold night air to return to their squadrons, or to make them sleep well, as the case may be; and as the voice of the orderly sergeant is heard going round with constantly repeated orders to "Get those lights out," the pilots and observers wander to their quarters to slumber peacefully, untroubled by thoughts of bombs and Boches; let them wait till the morrow.

"Sufficient unto the day is the evil thereof."

Chapter 13

Other Places—Other Methods

The R.F.C. in the East

The morning papers and Press generally give one the impression that there is a big war in Europe and a few little skirmishes in other parts of the world; consequently, few people realise that warfare in semi-civilised lands, waged in a very civilised manner, is at least as terrible as the affair in Europe, and very frequently has added risks and unpleasant conditions that make it desirable to be in France rather than East Africa, Mesopotamia, or even Salonica or Egypt.

I have little hesitation in saying that more men would prefer to transfer from these fronts to Flanders than would those men who have tasted each scene of activity like to return to the East. The "Call of the East" is all very well when unaccompanied by hardship and hourly danger of death; but when the heat, sand, mosquitos and biting insects innumerable are supplemented by the latest products of Essen and the flower of the Turkish Army supported by hordes of Bedouins and other semi-savage *denizens* of the desert thirsting to take one's life in the most horrible of ways, the East becomes a more unpleasant problem to tackle.

And though the army as a whole has received so little recognition for these vast conflicts against man and nature, the Royal Flying Corps might almost be non-existent for all that one sees of its doings in the Press. Not that the R.F.C. wishes or needs advertisement, but a word of recognition in due season encourages everyone.

The following happenings may serve to illustrate a few of the daily events which fall to the lot of the R.F.C. in the East—dangers which the pilots of the West may sleep without dreaming of.

One ever-present dread is the risk of a forced landing in the desert miles away from any outpost, either Turkish or British, without water, except for the small supply carried by all pilots who fly over the desert, without shelter of any kind from the burning sun which may send a man mad in a few hours, and without the slightest hope of ever reaching a habitation. No food is found in the desert, except a very little stunted shrub—only miles on miles of golden, undulating sand, broken by huge grey boulders and occasionally by the dried-up bed of a one-time river.

Nothing except the pitiless sun by day and the cold, ghastly moon and glittering stars by night. If figures are seen approaching it would probably be better to remain unseen, for a horrible death at the hands of these wandering tribesmen is all that may be expected. The only hope lies in the aeroplane which is always sent out to search for the machine which becomes overdue, the pilot landing and taking his stranded companion home as best he may, the crippled aeroplane being first set on fire.

One machine sent out on rescue work of this nature only arrived in time to see the end of a tragedy. An aeroplane returning from a desert reconnaissance was forced to land in the desert owing to engine trouble. The rescuing pilot located what seemed to be a wrecked aeroplane, and vanishing in the distance was a company of Bedouins mounted on camels. He landed and proceeded to the wreck which had been hacked to pieces with swords.

Many empty cartridge cases and a jammed Lewis gun with a half-expended drum still in position showed that the pilot and observer had put up a good fight. Confused tracks led away from the machine and at last ended by a large rock near which the mangled remains of two bodies were found, absolutely severed limb from limb and carved into pieces. Revolvers with empty cases still in the chambers lay at the foot of the rock where the two had made their last stand.

It will never be known how many of the enemy died first as the Bedouins carried their casualties off with them, but the many empty cases told their own tale, and no doubt exists that the lives of these two officers cost the enemy dearly. On the occasion of another forced landing an officer pilot and mechanic observer came down into the desert. The damage to the machine being beyond their resources to repair, they proceeded to wait for succour. At sundown the expected machine had not arrived, so they collected their water—a little over a gallon in all—fired the machine, and with the aid of a compass set out towards their lines.

For two days they travelled over the scorching sand, drinking their precious water drop by drop. At the end of that time the water was nearly all gone; with luck and all the remaining water one might possibly win through. That night the officer blew his brains out, leaving a note bidding his mechanic take all the water and go on. He died to save the man, who, it is consoling to think, in view of the great sacrifice, got through.

Another pilot was forced to descend in the sea near Gaza. He left his machine and swam ashore, only to be met by a Turkish patrol. Sooner than be taken prisoner he plunged into the sea again and landed a mile or so down the coast. As he was resting, he again saw Turks approaching, and once more took to the sea. That night he stayed on shore in peace, but in the morning on attempting, to resume his journey by land the presence of the enemy made him put out to sea.

Twice that day he attempted to land, and each time was soon forced to take the water again. At last, when he reached land for the third time towards evening, utterly exhausted and incapable of carrying on any longer, he fell in with an Australian patrol and was safely escorted back to the lines.

On one occasion it was found necessary to send out a small desert column of the Imperial Camel Corps and Royal Engineers to a remote town in the desert, at which place it was suspected that a hostile force was concentrating. A flight of the Royal Flying Corps was detailed to watch over this column and reconnoitre the surrounding country daily. When the column had arrived at its destination and was about to commence its main object—the destruction of a large number of wells—it was discovered that the wells were more numerous than had been supposed, and that insufficient gun-cotton had been carried by the column to enable them to do the necessary work of demolition.

To add to the difficulty the rations and water supply were very limited, and it was essential that the force should leave the town two days after it had reached there, thus not giving any time to obtain gun-cotton from the nearest depot. Had the wells not been destroyed the object of the column would not have been accomplished, and the expedition would have been a complete failure.

One of the reconnaissance machines seeing a signal from the column found a suitable spot in the vicinity and landed. The pilot hearing of the position volunteered with another pilot to fly back to the base and obtain 300 lbs. of gun-cotton that evening. The offer was accepted and the machines flew back, a journey of nearly 150 miles, to the base. The pilots obtained the necessary stores from Ordnance, placed them in the observers' seats of their machines, and flew out into the desert again.

If a forced landing had occurred it is possible that the pilots would not have been found even if they had succeeded in landing safely, which would have been doubtful owing to the rocky nature of the country. But both machines arrived safely at the destination. Half the wells were blown up the same evening and the work completed on the following morning. The column achieved its object, and another successful minor operation had been carried through.

Another episode in connection with the same operations occurred when an Australian trooper fell ill of typhoid. His condition was critical, and the Medical Officer reported that unless he reached hospital and received proper treatment within twenty-four hours, he had no hope of the man's life being saved. As the nearest hospital was over 100 miles away across barren and waterless desert it seemed impossible that the man could be given his chance.

As it happened an aeroplane landed at this spot to report on certain things seen on a reconnaissance. On hearing the condition of the sick man, the observer volunteered to remain with the desert column, and the pilot arranged to take the sick man as his passenger. The journey was accomplished safely, and the man reached hospital the same evening and his life was saved.

That East Africa can provide sensations the following incident shows.

A reconnaissance machine having failed to return, another pilot was sent out to look for it—rather a vain task in a country overgrown with forest and matted jungle growth. After a long search this officer noticed a large herd of elephants in the jungle, seemingly furiously attacking some object. He descended to within a few hundred feet before he grasped the fact that it was the missing aeroplane which was being torn to pieces by the infuriated beasts. Subsequently, when the whole story became known, it was found that the missing pilot had been forced to come down, his engine having given out, and he landed in the most accessible piece of jungle.

Whilst attempting to repair his engine—vain work, for he would not have been able to rise again—he was attacked by a herd of elephants who charged down upon the—to them—strange beast. The pilot wisely fled and took refuge in the nearest tree, from which position he watched the destruction of his beloved machine.

At last, the elephants, satisfied as to the death of the intruder, moved off, and the pilot determined to pass the night in the tree before attempting to reach camp in the morning. This, however, proved a vain determination, for with the departure of the elephants a leopard arrived, and he again had to move off, frightening the leopard away with his revolver.

All that night he wandered, steering by compass, and at early day was again disturbed and had to take refuge in a tree from lions. These left him in peace, and all went well until he reached a river, in swimming which he had a narrow escape from a crocodile. He then spread his clothes in the sun to dry, and fell asleep in the shade of the trees. He was awakened by the chattering of a crowd of baboons, which on his stirring himself made off into the forest, taking most of his clothes with them. For the rest of the day, he pressed steadily through the bush towards the aerodrome, tearing himself on thorns, suffering agonies from the heat, and in momentary dread of meeting more wild beasts.

Eventually, worn out, he fell asleep on the ground, where he was found by friendly natives who carried him into camp.

These and similar happenings are daily events in odd corners of the world.

Mesopotamia has furnished chances for many brave deeds which have been performed, amongst the most notable of which was a flight over a tremendous distance covered with hostile troops, from the British lines near Baghdad to the Russian forces in the neighbourhood of Kermanshah.

In India on the N.W. Frontier the R.F.C. has done invaluable work in the numerous little affairs with the hill tribes, and on at least one occasion a flight of aeroplanes has been the sole force used to disperse a native mob, the machine-guns from the air, aided by a few bombs, causing the hillmen to fly in disorder with many casualties.

Salonica, too, has been the scene of much aerial work, and the country has been of the very worst for the airman forced to descend. On this front co-operation with the French Flying Corps has been carried out to a very great extent. It is hard to single out instances for mention when so many notable deeds come to light.

At a certain place during the summer of 1915 was a rather quiet—in fact, unusually quiet for a Canadian—fellow who had been sent down to learn observing. Someone in authority had thought him not quite good enough for a pilot, but as he seemed keen on the air, he was given a chance of becoming an observer, and after he had gained experience in that way he might possibly be trained as a pilot. He was rather disappointed at the prospect of having to wait for perhaps a year before he took his ticket, but made the best of a bad job and contented himself with telling those who were stationed there with him what he would do when he was given his own machine to look after. He had thoroughly made up his mind to win the V.C. and possibly several other decorations, and his fellow officers were quietly amused at his confidence, though it was all without the slightest swank that he made these remarks.

Time went on, and those who learnt to fly during that summer forgot all about the Canadian who was becoming an observer. Some were killed, others became missing, and probably one and all had forgotten him, until one day the papers seemed suddenly to be filled with the doings of a Canadian airman, Captain Bishop who was none other than the observer who was not good enough to fly during 1915. The last time he was seen by the writer was in the R.F.C. Club, and he was wearing the ribbons of the V.C., D.S.O. and M.C. he had amply fulfilled the promises he had made to us in the summer two years before.

Among many wonderful deeds, probably his most thrilling was about the time of the great battle round Ypres during 1917, when he set out on his own to see how he could annoy the Huns. He began the day by patrolling the roads and canals and scattering any troops he could see by fire from his machine-gun. He then visited an aerodrome, and woke the Huns by dropping a few bombs on the hangars. Having thoroughly aroused them, he went further on and continued his game of annoying the enemy cavalry.

Then, by way of a change, he raced after a couple of enemy fighters which he saw in the distance, and after an exciting combat shot one down and chased off the other. Finding nothing else to do he returned to look at his doings on the aerodrome, and found that the machines were being brought out for the day's work. He promptly dropped a few bombs, and dived his machine, firing at as he did so. An aeroplane tried to get off to chase him away, but before it was well in the air, he shot it down and killed the observer.

Another machine tried to start up, but was stopped by a bomb before it could leave the earth. By this time the whole place was practically deserted so Bishop flew round firing his machine-gun in the hangars and then, all his ammunition expended, left for home. Not a bad beginning for the day's work, for he was out again before the evening came.

Another air V.C. was Sergeant Mottershead. During an aerial combat his machine was set on fire on the other side of the lines. It was hopeless to continue the combat, so he set his nose for home and tried to descend. He was in a pusher type of aeroplane, so the flames blew away from him, but the heat was intense. His observer, who was in a slightly better position, took the fire extinguisher and sprayed Mottershead and the burning machine, and gradually they descended. By the skill of the pilot, and because of his remarkable bravery and devotion to duty, the machine landed safely and the observer, Lieut. Gower, was saved, but Mottershead died almost immediately from his terrible burns.

These deeds can be multiplied indefinitely—indeed, a whole book could easily be filled with the brave efforts made by the officers and men of the Corps; but this book purports to be a slight description of the *work* of the Corps, and such a regiment needs no words to describe its prowess. By deeds it will gain its name, and so in the future it will keep it.

CHAPTER 14

The Storm

The pilot was young—not that that made him more noticeable amongst a corps of young men—and was about to go overseas for the first time. He waited at the depot from where so many pilots proceed overseas, and as he waited a great desolation swept over him. It would have been easier if he had been going over with a squadron of others, but he was going over alone to replace a casualty, and the feeling that he was to replace a dead man did not help to cheer him up.

All around him were aeroplanes at many types, big and small, scouts, fighters, and reconnaissance machines, all waiting to be taken over in the course of the next few days. He was taking a single-seater fighting 'plane, one of the best of the day, for he was a good pilot, and likely to do well.

As he waited for his machine to have the finishing touches put to it and the gun fitted, he thought of the times that had gone by, the early days of the war when he trained as an infantryman, the last days at home before his regiment—a jolly crowd—went over to the real thing, the days in the trenches, a memory of mud, water and anxious waiting, culminating in a rush across a bullet-swept piece of ground and a stinging pain in his arm—just a mere Blighty—and then, later, days of leave, the resolution to join the Flying Corps, the days of in-struction, his first crash—a ghastly memory that even now made him shudder to think how narrowly he had escaped death—and, lastly, his orders to proceed overseas to replace a casualty.

The last thought stung him; he did not like the idea of replacing a dead man. It was an ominous beginning. Would he be more success-ful than his forerunner, or was the sudden death on high reserved for him also? The idea chilled him, and fearful thoughts of "Archie," overwhelming odds of the enemy, and his machine on fire descending in a spinning nose-dive possessed him.

He pulled himself together and tried to drive his mind in another direction. To which squadron would he be sent? Would he find any of his old friends there? What would his first job be? And then his thoughts took that ghastly turn again, and he was awakened from his reverie by a voice informing him that his aeroplane was ready and his gun awaited a trial before being fitted.

As he walked towards his machine a new feeling of confidence took him in possession. He tried the gun, inspected his maps, tried the controls, settled himself comfortably in the seat and called "Contact." The roar of the engine thoroughly brought him back to his old self, and he felt the equal to any Hun who flew. As he sped over the aerodrome the feeling of confidence grew, and by the time he was circling to get his height he longed for his first conflict, and set his course for France.

It was gloriously fine, and the feel of the air gave him a joy of life which is only experienced by airmen. The sun shone warm on his face, and his pulse beat with the full vigour of youth. Far below the country passed by like a map—green fields, dark woods and white, winding roads. As he sped on, he kept his eye fixed on the railway line which was his guide, and his thoughts were the thoughts of the air.

Presently the sun ceased to shine, and he suddenly came upon thin, fleecy clouds, which hindered his view of the earth and the guiding rail, without entirely obscuring it. He descended a few hundred feet to gain a clearer view, but the sunshine was gone and the clouds close above him grew darker and gloomier. A few drops of rain showed on his windscreen, and suddenly a gust of wind shook the machine and drove a cutting squall of rain in his face. A minute later a fiercer cut was felt, and he saw hailstones dropping in his lap while his face smarted with the blows. Hastily taking a compass bearing of his course, he pushed up the nose of his machine and rose straight into the cloud.

Dark blackness surrounded him for a few minutes, and then the air grew clearer, the clouds grew fleecy, and a second later he emerged again into the warm sunshine. Below him rolled a mighty panorama of moving white billows, appearing exactly like animated cotton-wool. As far as he could see no break appeared in the sea of clouds, and he could only keep on his compass course until a gap occurred, which would enable him to see the ground and pick up his bearings. He kept steadily on, but the rolling clouds showed no signs of breaking, so he resolved to keep on his course for another half-hour, by which time he estimated he should be near his destination, when he could descend through the clouds, pick up his position, and finish his journey in the discomfort of the rainstorm.

A few minutes after he had taken this resolve he felt a difference in the air, a softer feel, like the feel of the sea, and concluded that he was over the Channel. So far so good. His calculations were correct, and provided he kept his course he should arrive at his journey's end without mishap.

Meanwhile the clouds grew thicker, and a sudden blinding light followed by a terrific roar convinced him that he was in the midst of a thunderstorm. A thunderstorm on earth is a terrifying enough spectacle, but when one becomes the centre of the turmoil it beggars description. To add to the pilot's discomfort his compass began to swing in an uncertain manner, and he realised that as a guide it was now useless, having been thrown out of action by the lightning.

Below him the clouds rolled and billowed like a rough sea, and blinding flashes of flame, alternating with crashing peals of thunder, showed him the progress of the storm. The half-hour which he had allowed himself was up, but it was useless to attempt to descend through such an inferno. His compass was useless, and his only way was to keep on as straight a line as possible until he was able to get within sight of earth, and then to pick up his bearings if possible, or land and inquire his whereabouts.

By the time the storm had died away behind him he had covered many miles, and at last, seeing a gap in the clouds, he dived for it and came again in sight of earth. He searched his map in a vain effort to find his position, but could not recognise the area over which he was flying. In the distance was a large town, and for this he made, being sure that when over it he would be able to see some feature of the country clearly marked on the map, and so get on his course once more.

A very few minutes sufficed to take him to the town in question, and he circled round to look at it thoroughly. Suddenly, without the slightest warning, his machine pitched violently, and a cloud of smoke appeared a short distance to his side. Before he could make up his mind what this meant another puff appeared a little closer, and again his machine jerked against the controls. A third puff right in front of him, and several holes in his planes caused him to realise that he was being shelled by "Archie," and he hastily sheered off from the uncomfortable spot followed by the venomous puffs of shells from a gun far below.

Where he was, he still had not the faintest idea, but he had seen quite enough to understand that he was miles off his course and over enemy territory. Realising that he was too far north, and knowing that his compass was useless from the effects of lightning, he turned sharp to the right and headed as far as he could judge to the south, in the hope of crossing the line and eventually descending at a British aerodrome. He had got over the lines sooner than he anticipated, and as he was not exactly looking for trouble, thought that the nearest route for safety was the best that he could follow.

He was not, however, to be allowed to proceed along his course unmolested, and a spot hovering above him caused him to understand that if he would reach his lines in safety, he would have to fight for it. Hastily jamming on a drum of ammunition—he thanked his luck then that he had tried his gun before leaving England—he watched for his foe to attack. Though he could not yet distinguish the marks on the planes of the machine above him, he knew without the slightest doubt that it was piloted by an enemy, and prepared to receive it as such.

While he waited for the attack to begin, he wondered who his opponent might be. Was he a pilot new to the game like himself, or was he a veteran with a score of aerial combats to his credit?

His thoughts were cut short by the enemy suddenly diving at him. By a great effort he kept on his course for a few seconds that seemed like minutes, and then, when he judged the right moment had come, wheeled round to the left out of the course of his foe. He saw the machine shoot by, spurts of flame coming through the propeller, and realised that for the present he was safe. Below him the machine flattened out and commenced to climb for another attack.

Now was the moment for him to become the aggressor, and he wheeled and flew at the Hun. Fifty yards away he pressed the trigger of his Lewis and saw his opponent bank, side slip and recover as he got out of the line of fire. Once again, he tried to climb to the attack, and again was driven off; and then, either sickening of the attack or scenting an easier victim, sheered off and retired into his own country. The pilot did not follow. His one thought was to find where he was, and land in safety at a British aerodrome.

During the combat he had again lost his direction, and could only guess that he was going towards the lines by going in the opposite direction to that taken by his late opponent.

At last, he again sighted machines, and by their build knew them to be British. Whether they were coming from their aerodromes or returning after a raid he could not tell, but noticing the excellent formation of their flight decided that they must be proceeding on a raid, so he continued in the opposite direction to their line of flight. He had long ago discarded his map as useless, but a river ahead of him caused him to look at the map again, and at last he picked up several landmarks and found himself. He was miles over his destination, and far behind the lines in the enemy's country. However, the knowledge of his position cheered him up, and provided he could cross the lines he now felt safe.

Thinking of his position brought to his mind his petrol tanks, now nearing exhaustion, and all the possibilities of a forced landing in the German lines came home to him. As he pondered this possibility, he saw many miles off the jagged lines of trenches which he had known so well and hated so cordially in days gone by. Now he thought of them as a haven of refuge, and longed for the security of a funk-hole. Would his supply of fuel last long enough to enable him to cross those dirty black marks and reach safety, or would he be forced to descend within a few miles of his own countrymen? His reverie was interrupted by the violent lurch of his machine, which he this time at once recognised as "Archie." Putting his nose down, twisting and wheeling like a snipe, he shamelessly bolted for home.

Those black jagged marks coming momentarily nearer meant safety to him, and his whole mind was possessed with the one idea of crossing them before his petrol gave out or a stray shot from the guns hit a vital spot and finished his career before it had well begun. Each second seemed an age, and each shot seemed closer than the last, but little by little he approached his goal, nose down, engine thundering, the whole machine flying at a speed far in advance of any for which it had been designed. Closer and closer he crept; he was nearly over, and "Archie" was already beginning to slacken, when his engine gave a warning splutter, misfired, picked up, and finally ceased to fire.

Mechanically he watched the propeller slow down, and his mind almost ceased to act. To have struggled so far and worked so hard to miss his goal by inches! It was hard luck. Unseeingly he passed over the trenches, so low that had he noticed he might have seen the men who were in them. He passed the support trenches and suddenly came to himself with a jerk to realise that he was over the trenches and safe.

All he had to do was land.

Ahead was a field which he thought he might just reach. He cleared the hedge by inches, flattened out, and bumped to a standstill within a few yards of its far boundary. He saw people coming towards him, and pulled himself together to receive them. He was dimly conscious of friendly voices inquiring as to his damage, and smiled faintly to reassure them before the strain and fatigue of the day overcame him, and he allowed himself to fade off into a peaceful and profound faint.

CHAPTER 15

The Growth of the R.F.C.

It may not come amiss at this point to say a little about the growth of the Air Service, from its inception to the present time.

Before 1912 the Royal Flying Corps as a distinct unit did not exist, it being merely a unit of the Royal Engineers—the Balloon Company B.E. On June 6, 1912, however, the authorities decided that the time had come to commence forming an Air Service in earnest, and the Balloon Company was given the title of the Royal Flying Corps, with military and naval wings.

At that time very few aeroplanes were in possession of the government, and comparatively few were in private hands, the military authorities specialising in dirigible airships of rather primitive type, and a few of slightly better design bought from foreign countries.

The first all-British airship to make anything like a really successful flight was the famous *Nulli Secundus*—a most perfect imitation of a flying sausage—which aroused wild cheers and vast enthusiasm on its trial flight over Farnborough Common in the presence of crowds of people and representatives of nearly every paper in the British Islands. Later editions of the same type followed, and specimens of the *Parseval*, *Clement Bayard* and *Lebaudy* were bought from other countries.

The naval authorities, too, built an airship to their own design— the ill-fated *Mayfly* which broke its back before the trial trip. Kites also were popular at this time, long strings of them supporting a basket in which sat an observer who ascended and descended along an iron cable governing the velocity of his descent by means of a brake on the winch.

The first aeroplane, as distinct from airship, was built by the late Mr. F. S. Cody when he was in the employ of the Government. It may also be noted that the kites so largely used at one time were of his design, so that he may be styled the "Father of British military aviation." Those who witnessed the trials of his first heavier than air machine on the Swan Plateau at Farnborough are not likely to forget it, with its numbers of tapes tied to the struts and trailing edge of the planes streaming out in the wind.

This machine did nothing more than taxi over the ground at a fair speed, but when modifications were made it rose from the ground on several occasions, though nothing like a really good flight was ever attaint. It was not until Cody had ceased to be employed by the government that he produced a really efficient machine, and it is to the everlasting discredit of those responsible that more help was not given to him in the early days.

After this, when the possibility of flight in a machine designed in England was at last sufficiently demonstrated to the authorities, aeroplanes were acquired for the use of the R.F.C. and stations were established in various parts of Great Britain-Farnborough, Montrose, Gosport and Lark Hill being the most important. Machines were very scarce and of what would now be considered most primitive types.

Few opportunities were given to officers to learn to pilot these precious aeroplanes—Farmans, Caudrons and Box-Kites for the most part-and nearly all the instructional work was done at civilian schools, the Short School at Lark Hill being one of the most popular, and supplying most of the pilots. Later the Central Flying School was formed at Upavon, where both naval and military officers received instruction before being passed into a squadron for service.

On July 1, 1914, the Royal Naval Air Service was formed, and ceased to be merely the naval wing of the Royal Flying Corps. At this time, however, and for some considerable time afterwards, the Central Flying School continued to be used for both naval and military officers. Shortly after this division the war broke out, and the infant services proceeded to prove their practical

It is interesting to note the performances of machines with which the Corps was then equipped, and consider their performances compared with those in use at the front at the present time. Perhaps the best machine then owned by the British Army was the B.E., of which several types were in use. This machine, fitted with a 70-h.p. Renault engine was capable of flying about 65 miles per hour at the best, and it is worth while noting that very few were fitted with this engine, the 80-h.p. Gnome being used in considerably higher numbers.

Both the Henri and Maurice Farmans did ten miles an hour less, as did the Caudrons and Shorts. This exhausts the list of biplanes used then by the British Amy, but in addition they possessed a few monoplanes of such types as Bleriot, Deperdussin, Flanders, Nieuport and Martinsyde.

As regards climb, 3,000 feet in ten minutes was thought to be quite good, if not a very startling performance. The only machine having any degree of natural stability was the B.E., and such points as fighting capacity were entirely neglected. A machine flying at anything over 3,000 feet was considered perfectly safe from gunfire, and as there was no other method of offensive in the air the pilots of that period were practically safe as long as the engine did not give out. At the present time, with machines being brought down from 20,000 feet by antiaircraft fire, and aerial fighting reduced to a fine art with everything new in the way of machine-guns and patent sights, the lot of the pilot on active service is far from pleasant.

In pre-war days much talk and a good deal of thought was spent in considering the war possibilities of the aeroplane, and the general conclusion reached was that while the new arm would be of incalculable assistance as a reconnoitring force, its sphere of utility would end there, with the exception of possibly a little bombing as opportunity afforded. The very fact that the average machine could not encompass a flight of more than about three and a half hours, and had therefore a radius of action of only about 130 miles, seemed to preclude the possibility of organised bombing raids on a large scale, and aerial fitting was almost undreamt of, though experiments had been carried out at Brooklands with a light gun fixed to an aeroplane. Also, the reliability of any engine used was so poor that machines were being constantly held up on that account.

As regards the actual growth of the Corps, in August, 1914, there were about one hundred officers and a thousand other ranks, with perhaps eighty serviceable machines. At the present time one is safe in saying that the total personnel would have been a very considerable addition to the original Expeditionary Force.

During the first months of the war the function of the Royal Flying Corps was largely to reconnoitre for the various armies and reporting position and movements of the enemy. But there is no doubt that the Corps largely helped to save the Mons army, and probably the whole of the Western Front during the critical period in August, 1914.

If it had not been for the aeroplane scouts who brought in confirmation of the report that General Smith-Dorrien was faced by not three German Divisions as had been thought, but by three whole Army Corps, it is possible that the whole of the British Army might have been wiped out, the Germans might have reached Paris, and probably the whole aspect of the war would have been changed, and certainly not to the advantage of the Allies.

The Germans had far more machines available than the Allies and a far better method of organisation, so that in addition to the reconnaissance work they also took on themselves the spotting for their artillery—hence, in a great measure, the immense superiority of the enemy's gunfire in the early days. Not only were their machines more numerous, but they had also better and more reliable engines, and a larger and more highly trained personnel.

About the beginning of 1915 the R.F.C. began to receive some of the new types of machines, and at once began to assert their superiority over the enemy. Aerial combats were by this time becoming common, if not the everyday experiences they were to become shortly. In reply to our new types the Germans brought out the famous Fokker, and brought down a considerable number of our aeroplanes before the pilots had realised the manoeuvre by which it was achieved. The Fokker was an obvious imitation of the Morane monoplane as used by the French, but it was specially strengthened in order to fit it for the special form of attack practised by the pilots of these machines, as described in Chapter 10. Large numbers of our machines were destroyed in this manner, until British pilots realised that the attack was always managed in exactly the same way, and took steps to amend their own flying.

With the advent of the F.E. type of machine the British swept the Germans off the whole of the battle front, and by the autumn of 1916 it was an exceedingly rare occurrence to see a German flyer over the line.

The autumn of 1916, too, saw the advent of yet another form of aerial warfare—the contact patrol, in which low-flying machines assisted the infantry, reporting every small movement of the enemy, and even flying close over the trenches, helped to demoralise them by means of machine-gun fire.

The struggle for air supremacy still continues; at one time the enemy produces a machine which is superior to anything the Allies can put against it, and this is quickly overcome by some new British or French machine. Speed, climb, flexibility, ease of manoeuvring, weight lifting, clearness of vision and range of action all go to make a machine the superior of its rivals, and the human element is the most important factor of all. This in a great measure accounts for the success of the Allies in the air.

It has been noticed that at the beginning of hostilities 70 miles per hour was a high speed, and that a climb of 3,000 feet in ten minutes was considered a very fair performance. Now let us notice some of the characteristics of the latest machines used in warfare. It is safe to say that the majority of machines used for fighting purposes can easily do 100 miles an hour under adverse conditions, carrying two passengers, guns and ammunition, and a full load of petrol and oil, and many types will do considerably more—anything up to 130 miles per hour—whilst the fast single-seaters can fly level at anything from 120 to 150 miles per hour.

The heavier bombing and reconnaissance machines, carrying big loads and capable of operating over a large radius, will average a steady 90 to 100 miles per hour. The climbing capacity of some of the latest types is almost incredible, 10,000 feet being reached in five minutes or thereabouts. What will be achieved in the near future is beyond conjecture.

In August, 1914, the sole work of aircraft was connected with reconnaissance, with a very small amount of spotting, but now the sphere of activities has become vastly enlarged. It includes bombing raids, photography of a most marvellous character, exposures being made that show the most minute details of trench work far more accurately than they can be seen by the human eye, fighting singly and in grand aerial battles in which as many as a hundred machines have been engaged, artillery observation of the highest accuracy, enabling long-range guns to fire at invisible objects and have the results of each shot signalled to them by wireless almost as soon as the explosion takes place, to supplement infantry in driving the enemy out of trenches by machine-gun fire—in fact, in almost every way in which any branch of the army can make itself felt. The R.F.C. has even usurped the place of the A. S.C. by carrying stores into Kut!

Will the war of the future be entirely waged by the men and machines of the air?

CHAPTER 16

Back to Blighty

When the pilot sighted his prey some miles off, he thought of little else but getting within range of his adversary, who thinking discretion the better part of valour opened out his engine and headed for home. Unfortunately for him, however, he had some way to go, and the pilot, alone in his fast little fighting scout, rapidly overhauled the German machine. At last, seeing that escape was hopeless, the Boche turned and manoeuvred to get at the British machine.

He was in a rather clumsy biplane, and was soon outgeneralled by his opponent, who poured in a drum from his machine-gun, rapidly changed the empty canister for another fully charged one, and again attacked. After a few rounds a spurt of flame burst from the Boche machine, and the whole fabric rapidly caught fire. The pilot was seen hanging forward helplessly in his seat, and then the blazing mass plunged down to earth.

Unluckily, the British pilot was so engaged in watching where the wrecked Hun fell that he had eyes for nothing else, or he would have seen the approach of another machine at a higher altitude. When this aeroplane was a thousand feet over the British one, it suddenly dived and loosed off a drum of ammunition. The British pilot was made aware of the presence of his enemy by a sudden sharp dart of pain in his leg. He saw his adversary dive out of range far below, realised what had happened, and decided to turn for home. One leg was helpless, and he was losing blood rapidly, but he could manage his machine and hoped to last out.

Once he sighted an enemy 'plane in the distance, but it did not attack, and gradually he neared the line. He was growing weaker, and the pain in his leg grew greater, but he set his teeth and determined to stick it.

At length he saw his aerodrome in the distance, the hangars showing as tiny specks thousands of feet below, and he throttled down his engine to descend. Lower and lower he came until the aerodrome was just beneath him. He could hardly last out any longer, but force of habit made him turn into the wind and land. He had a dim notion of shutting off his engine and flattening out, and then the pain and weakness overcame him, and he drifted into the unknown.

His companions at the aerodrome had seen him land, and thought there was nothing wrong. He had landed properly up-wind—perhaps the landing was just a trifle bumpy—and run along until the machine stopped. Mechanics ran out to start up his engine again and bring the aeroplane in, and naturally the pilot remained in his seat to manipulate the controls.

It was only when the mechanic called out "Switch off" to the pilot and received no answering assurance, that he looked round. The pilot's face, hidden in cap and mask, betrayed nothing, but the limp figure hanging forward in the nacelle and the blood trickling from the machine told their tale, and very soon the ambulance was on the scene, the wounded man gently lifted from his seat and placed on a stretcher.

Probably the moving aroused him from his stupor, for he opened his eyes and, smiling wanly at his surrounding companions, said: "Anyhow, I strafed the blighter." He then again relapsed into unconsciousness. Naturally, his fellow-officers concluded that he had sunk the Boche who attacked him; they did not know until afterwards that it had been a fight against odds.

Despite the jolting of the ambulance, he did not wake again until his wound had been dressed and he was safely in bed in the Casualty Clearing Station. For obvious reasons officers of the Flying Corps usually miss the Dressing Station to which infantrymen first go on being wounded in the trenches. He looked around and tried to move into a more comfortable position, but the pain in his leg reminded him of what had happened and he groaned. The groan brought a sister to him, who asked if he felt better now.

The pilot smiled. "Better!" He inquired where he was and what would be done with him, and was told that he would probably be taken to the base by the next hospital train.

"When will that be?" he asked.

"Oh, in four or five days' time, I expect. We had one train in yesterday, so there will not be one for a few days."

He looked around him for the comfortable hospital ward of which he had so often heard. Instead, he saw the stone floor, whitewashed walls and barred windows of the old town prison, now a hospital. Hardly cheering, yet neat and clean, if nothing else. From patients suffering with minor troubles and nerves, who were able to be up and about, he heard more details of the place; of the cobbled yard surrounded by high stone walls and iron-barred windows, wherein they took exercise; of the solitary confinement cells now used as store-rooms, and the huge gates and flanking towers, showing the devices for fixing and lowering portcullis and drawbridge, and the remains of the moat, for, in earlier times, before the place became a prison, it had been one of the forts defending the town hard by. Fort, prison, hospital; the old grey walls could tell many a story.

Slowly the days passed—days in which the sole events were the painful dressings of his wound, and the agony of a chance touch of the broken bone. These were the happenings by which the hours were counted, if we except his anxiety with regard to his kit, which at length had arrived safely.

At last, one evening the welcome news came that a hospital train would leave for the base next day, and wild excitement reigned in the officers' ward. Getting to the base was the first real step for Blighty—that magic place which is so hard to reach. Two others were marked for the base, and next morning all three were placed on the stretchers of the ambulance, and bumped over the *pavé* to the station. The agony of those cobbled roads to broken bones is horrible. Be the driver ever so careful, every bump causes the fractured bones to grate and the patient to groan, but all rides have an end.

Eventually the station was reached, and another move was made into the waiting train, the pilot being placed on a lower berth and warmly covered with blankets, a cradle keeping the weight of the clothes off his injured leg. All around him were other officers, sitting or lying about the ward—for the carriage was one large ward—and through the corridor could be seen a vision of more bunks, one over the other, crowded with men broken in the war, whilst up and down moved the figures of nurses, doctors and orderlies.

Some of the men near him were sitting up playing cards; they were class three, or sitting cases, and consisted chiefly of "nerves." He, of course, was a stretcher case, and deserving of every attention. On the wall beside him he noticed the letters G.E.R., and idly wondered if he had ever travelled in the old coach in England before its dividing walls were knocked down to make one large room, and it was moved from its native East Anglia to the fields of France.

The train at last moved off, and as he lay there speculating, the nurse, whom he had seen moving among the recumbent figures, approached him, placed a thermometer in his month and took his wrist in her fingers. She noted down the results, asked him if he was comfortable, and moved on to the next.

A doctor passed and gave him a smile, and continued his round; he had many patients and no time to waste on those who did not immediately need his professional skill. Soon another nurse approached, not to take temperatures, but bringing an armful of books and magazines to while away the time, for hospital trains travel slowly for the sake of their patients.

The next incident on the journey was lunch. Having ascertained that he could manage to eat something, an orderly presented him with a flat board to act as a table, and a cup of soup to commence with. In due course he received a civilised meal, well cooked and seemingly impossible to produce on a hospital train. However, it was there, and was eaten, and afterwards he fell asleep.

When he awoke the train was at a standstill, and the sitting cases were already leaving. His turn came at last, and he was again placed on a stretcher, carried in front of an officer who referred to a list, and without delay named him for a certain hospital. There was no bustle, no confusion; everyone knew his business and everything ran smoothly. He was placed with others in an ambulance and whirled away out of the station, up the hill, and finally arrived at the base hospital—or rather a hospital forming one of a group at the base.

At the hospital the same order and lack of confusion was noticed as elsewhere, and the pilot was carried straight upstairs, placed in bed again and made comfortable. He learnt that this particular hospital was run by an Englishwoman who had married an American engaged in the production of munitions. All patients, whether officers or "other ranks," who came under her care were given the best of everything.

The pilot was astonished to receive a dinner such as he would expect in a London hotel, but hardly hoped to find in a hospital at the front. He was asked by the head waiter—for one could hardly call him an orderly—what he would drink. This was such a surprise—used as he had been in the Clearing Station to cold water—that he gave no answer, and was promptly supplied with some excellent white wine. Altogether he had landed in clover

Presently a doctor appeared, not to inspect his newly dressed wounds, but to "have a look at him." He told the pilot that he would go over to Blighty in a few days, when he had rested from his long journey in the train, as it would not hurt him to travel, and they were expecting a large convoy of wounded who would fill every available bed, for at this time the second phase of the Battle of the Somme was commencing. Thus, cheered up the pilot fell into a doze—there were three other beds in the ward, but the occupants were all up—and was only awakened by the day sister going off duty and visiting him to see if all was well.

Then his fellow patients turned in, and the night sister arrived. He had a vision of a sweet face, full of sympathy and tenderness; a face untouched by the professional hardness acquired by some nurses, but not lacking in firmness; her small hands were slender yet capable—altogether she seemed the very perfection of nurses. Small wonder, then, that he slept easily, and smiled in his sleep when she visited him on her rounds. He awoke early, and found her busy near him.

That day passed as in a dream; he only lived for two things—Blighty and the night. He may have been very impressionable in his state of health, but at times he thought he would prefer to remain in France and not go back to Blighty. But alas for his hopes; that evening a large convoy arrived; the sick and wounded filled the hospital—even the floor was covered with improvised beds and stretchers, and doctors and nurses hurried about, easing pain where possible or dulling it with the sense-slurring syringe. When the pressure had eased a little the sister in charge came in to him with labels; one she fixed to the coverlet of his bed, two others she left by his chart. She said nothing, but smiled to him.

"What are you labelling me for, Sister?" he asked.

"Oh! You're for Blighty sometime tomorrow morning. The boat may leave any time between five and nine o'clock." Still smiling, she left him.

When at last he was really bound for home in a few hours' time, all lingering doubts as to whether nurse and France were better soon vanished. When the night sister came on duty, he received her with a beaming smile, very different from the sentimental grin he had obviously bestowed on her. Blighty was best—better than all things.

He was rather excited that night and seemed unlikely to sleep, so his divinity showed his practical side by giving him aspirin and hot milk, and he soon went off. Next morning, he was awakened early,

ATTACKING AN AIRSHIP

and found an orderly waiting to help on his tunic.

"What's up now?" he demanded.

"Ambulance's waiting, sir," replied the man, and it needed little more to persuade him to don his tunic, even though he was labelled from either shoulder strap like a piece of luggage. He was placed on a stretcher once more, well wrapped up, bade a fond *adieu* to the fair night sister, and was whirled away through the cold morning mist to the waiting hospital ship. He was carried on board, and stretcher and all was lowered into the vessel.

The crossing was luckily fine, and the journey similar in many respects to that on the train. England was reached at last, and he was gently transferred from the ship to a waiting train, and carried up to London. On the journey he was inspected by a Medical Officer, and marked down for a certain place. When the train finally stopped at London, he was soon placed once more in the waiting ambulance and taken to the hospital.

The waiting crowd that assembles to watch the unloading of hospital trains cheered noisily; they threw cigarettes, chocolates and flowers into the open ambulance; men raised their hats and women threw kisses. He was taken to a large London hospital, with long wards and symmetrically arranged beds, and here, surrounded by companions of all regiments from many parts of the line, he prepared for a long rest. A wound like his would take some months to heal, and there he would stay until able to walk a little.

★★★★★★★★★★★★

Three months later he left the hospital and, by train and boat, journeyed to Osborne, the home of Queen Victoria in the Isle of Wight, which was presented as a convalescent home to the Army and Navy by King Edward VII. He was surprised to find it looking so little like a hospital. Except for the Red Cross flying from the central tower, there was nothing to show what it was. He was received at the door by a lady dressed in white, who showed him upstairs to his bedroom. From her manner he guessed she was the matron, though she did not wear the grey uniform and red cape and cuffs to which he was accustomed.

Downstairs he met other officers, mostly looking hale and well, though a few limped on crutches; in the smoking-room were others reading and talking; from the billiard-room came the click of balls; nowhere did he see an orderly, nowhere a uniformed nurse. The whole place resembled a West-End club favoured by officers of both services. He dined in a manner which reminded him that he was off hospital diet again, and finally went up to his room, undressed, and sat in a dressing-gown before the fire to muse. Decidedly Osborne was a good place to come to.

Next day he was able to see outside the place. Below the front of the building the gardens descended, terrace on terrace, each with its fountains and statues. Sheltered recesses with easy chairs encouraged the convalescents out of doors, and all around stretched a wide-spreading park. Trees of different climates flourished in the mild air, and up a fine specimen of a cork tree ran a squirrel. In the distance, at the end of a long avenue, sparkled the sea, grey-blue in the autumn sunshine. He was not strong enough yet to go on to the golf links, but he could see others playing a round. The whole place had an air of peace and quietness, a complete rest from all to do with the war, and the atmosphere had a sweet softness about it that was good to lungs so long accustomed to the smell of iodine and ether.

There was a room specially set apart for such as he—a chamber full of many weird appliances for restoring wasted muscles, and in here for an hour a day strength was gradually rubbed back into his injured leg. Each day he could walk better, and he soon got as far as the sea and into the lovely woods which border it.

Cowes, nearby, was his next effort—a little town of dirty, narrow streets, presenting few attractions except a small and poor kinema. Having seen Cowes, he preferred to keep to the grounds, play billiards and read. Friends visited him, and as he grew stronger, he visited other parts of the island.

Two or three times a week the House Governor and his assistant held medical boards and numbers of the inmates were sent off, cured, for a few weeks' leave before rejoining their units. At last, his turn came and he was sent off for a month's leave. A subsequent board at the end of that time passed him fit for light duty, and in due course he reported at the War Office, after having been sick for nearly eight months.

With the Royal Flying Corps on Active Service. The adjustment of a heavy bomb on a de Haviland. A Nieuport fighter is seen in the background, apparently ready to start as a guard to the bombing machine.

CHAPTER 17

The Future of Aviation

Immense as have been the strides that flying has made during the last few years—especially since August, 1914—the future abounds with many possibilities so far undreamt of as well as developments along expected and normal lines. It is impossible to place any limit on the developments of such a means of locomotion, speed, and general utility as the aeroplane has already become, and it is equally impossible to prophesy the limits to which its uses may be applied.

Probably the first development which may be expected will be along the lines of rapid communication between one part of the world and another, and it is fairly safe to assume that the postal authorities of the Powers will be among the first to make use of this method of communication. At present it takes at least three weeks for a letter to be delivered in India from the time of its posting in England, but with aeroplanes, flying at the very moderate speed of 100 miles an hour, the time should be reduced to a very few days, and with the developments which are possible we may live to hear of the inauguration of a daily mail to many of our colonies.

Aerodromes along the trade routes will be the first problem to tackle, for the most perfect of machines must land at times to replenish its supply of fuel, and the most enduring of pilots feels the strain of flying for several hours on end. This should prove no difficulty in regards communication with most parts of the earth; but certain places, such as New Zealand, many miles away from the next land will have to be thought of in a different manner.

Seaplanes have amply demonstrated their ability to alight even on a fairly rough sea, but the question of petrol storage depots and repair parks must not be overlooked. On land this will be a perfectly simple matter, for at each aerodrome supplies of fuel and oil can be stored and a few mechanics be stationed to look after any machines which may land and undertake any small repairs that may be necessary, but at sea is this possible?

The fate of the unfortunate postman who has a forced descent at sea through lack of petrol or through some minor defect to his machine, miles away from any land and off the track of the steamship routes, is terrible to contemplate, for even the most experienced airman is liable to these things, and shipwreck can hardly be considered a fair aviator's risk. Perhaps the difficulty may be overcome by inaugurating a system of depot ships along the air routes, each ship equipped with wireless to receive the S.O.S. of any shipwrecked aviator, and a few mechanics to repair the damages which prevent the machine from continuing its journey.

Weight again is a serious consideration when thinking of an aerial post. We read of huge liners being lost with thousands of bags of mails on board; no aeroplane yet built would carry 100 bags, though possibly this, is merely a thing to await for in the natural course of events. Again, the greater frequency of the mail would diminish the number of bags to be carried at one time, though the frequency of transit would probably cause a greater amount of correspondence to be written. We may confidently assert, however, that the weight difficulty will be overcome before many years have passed.

Reliability is another factor which needs consideration. The essential factors of a mail service are speed and reliability. Speed we may safely assume to be one of the appurtenances of the future. Will reliability also figure largely in the aerial service to come? At present many thousands of miles are flown for every forced landing, and the average grows greater daily. Witness the number of miles flown per fatal accident. In 1908, the rate was about 300 miles for each life.

By 1910, the mileage had increased ten times, and at present it is safe to assume, from figures issued by the American Government, that at least 500,000 miles are flown for each death; this, of course, does not include casualties due to the war, though it does include deaths while training, deaths which will decrease largely in numbers when the necessity for a huge and hurried output of pilots ceases to exist. Under these conditions it is safe to assume that aerial transport will be reliable enough for the mail of the future.

Cost needs consideration also. At present it would be absolutely impossible to carry letters by air at the rate at which they are carried

British Aeroplane at Kut

by train and sea, and it is very doubtful whether it will be possible to do so in the future. For the aerial post to be a financial success it would be necessary to charge at a high rate for the transmission of letters—a rate which would also preclude the possibility of the voluminous letter-writer flooding the post with letters which would occupy valuable space.

Ordinary mails and parcels would continue to be carried by train and mail-boat, but those letters which were of great importance and urgency could be carried by the aerial post. By this means business matters would receive attention much sooner than could otherwise be arranged, to the benefit of the people concerned and the country generally.

Apart from the postal side of the question, the travel view-point must be considered. In these days thousands are deterred from broadening their outlook on account of the difficulties attendant on moving from one place to another. Changes, especially with baggage, long journeys by night with their accompanying discomforts, wearisome hours in stuffy railway carriages, the awful sensations of sea-sickness, and the many other discomforts endured by the traveller of these days will be dispensed with.

A journey will be made without changing at many junctions, the traveller will not be worried with constant fears as to the safety of his baggage, and the time will be spent in the fresh air with the whole earth being rolled by in an immense panorama below. One difficulty which arises is that in connection with the Customs officials of the countries passed over, but doubtless international legislation will soon find a means of surmounting this by no means insurmountable difficulty.

Sport, pleasure, business, warfare—all will find their arena in the air. The rules for travel will need altering, as well as those pertaining to the more strenuous pleasures of life. Even in these days of comparative freedom in the upper regions collisions are not unheard of, and in the time to come, with the air as full of aeroplanes as the streets are full of taxicabs at the present time, one must expect to hear of many fatalities. Before such happenings become general the rules of the air will need revision.

I say revision, for it is not generally realised that rules do exist at the present time governing the movements of meeting machines, and that all is not left to the impulses of individual pilots. Kipling in one of his stories tells of air lanes—different levels which are to be kept by different types of machines. Doubtless this is the most feasible method of overcoming the traffic difficulty, and we shall speak of the 5,000-foot level as being reserved for the mail-planes, the 7,000-foot level as the place where one proceeds to take an airing, with higher or lower levels reserved for the cargo-plane, the aerial-taxi, or the sporting single-seater.

Landing-places present a very real difficulty at present, when the average machine needs a fairly level place at least 200 yards long in which to rise and land in safety. Common landing-grounds would partly solve the difficulty, but only partly. The real solution to the problem lies in the helio-copter, or some other device for enabling a machine to rise and land almost in the perpendicular. Thus, instead of being dropped at one's door, the landing will be effected on the housetop, and crowds of machines will be seen rising from the housetops of Mayfair—or wherever the society locality lies in those days—when the fashionable hour arrives.

The aerial policeman of the future will doubtless be a busy man, and will need to be a first-rate pilot if he is to stop the flight of fugitives from justice or the smuggling which will be so easily managed in the early days, and preserve the rule of the road whilst taking the numbers of machines which are flying at the wrong levels to the danger of the public. Certificates must be granted to all those who wish to drive their own machine, and would-be pilots must be rigorously examined before licences are issued, and at frequent intervals in order to ensure their absolute fitness to fly a machine. Eventually, doubtless, the aeroplane will be managed so simply and safely that this examination will become unnecessary, but under present conditions the rule must be rigorously enforced.

It is impossible to say to what lengths flying may be carried in the future. As a sporting machine nothing in the world beats an aeroplane, and its reputation in this respect is not likely to decrease. Even now, many times, hares have been shot from machines flying low, and if hares, why not partridges and pheasants? What can be more exciting than the prospect of following a gaggle of geese into their own element, and securing a bag which would make the best shot of these days blush with shame.

War of the future, too, will almost certainly be waged in the air in entirety. Aerial blockades, aerial bombardments, aerial barrages —all these will form essential manoeuvres in the next war. Have we not seen their advent in the present struggle?

Many problems confront aviation in the years to come, but the victory for the aeroplane is assured, and speed, mobility and low cost at production with a high degree of reliability are sure to win in the end.

War in the Air Tales

The Death Harvest of the Dastard Zeppelin

By A. G. Hales

Paris.

From boyhood to manhood, I have loved peace, yet some perverse fate has always dragged me where storms and tempests are loosened. I had a heaven—once—within the circle of a woman's arms. The grey rider came and left me desolate.

And yet I love to look on the happiness of others. The sweetest picture in the world to me is the living picture of a man with his household idols around him; his wife with her foot upon the rocker of a cradle; his children clustering round him in the firelight's glow; his day's work done; his sweat and toil repaid by the all-compelling glances of his mate—his woman, his partner in joy and sorrow, victory and defeat.

God bless the women! They are the salt of the earth, as man is the sweat of the brown earth that cradled us all. It is the women I feel for now—not only the British women, but the women of the world. This is their hour of despair; they are drinking the broth brewed from tears, and eating the unleavened cakes baked on the breasts of sorrow. Heaven pity them, for they walk on thorns and every step is marked with blood.

We do not value them sufficiently in peace time, but if we be men, we can die for them in time of war. This is our privilege.

THE ANGUISH OF OLD WOMEN

Come here, where war's hellish footprints are pressed into the soil; come here, where the earth is red with good, brave blood, and you will know what womanhood stands for. Here we are on the crater of Hades, and it is the women who are making the men great. Yet how the women are suffering! The old grey wife clutches the children at her heart and holds them. They are bone of her bone, though she never bore them; but she bore the father who begat them or the mother who brought them forth, and their blood is her blood.

She listens in the watches of the night when even the mothers and the fathers sleep, for age is long-suffering and anguish tears at the withered hearts. She watches—she waits—she listens—as you in England would watch and wait and listen if the German devil got possession of the Channel coast, and were free to let his airships loose upon your cities.

The night passes, the children rise from their sleeping and run about their play in chubby beauty and all the recklessness of young life that knows not sorrow or pain or dread. The mother takes up the granddame's burden; every sound makes her start and grip her breasts, as if a knife had stabbed her.

She is full of the pain of unknown things. The joy of her man, the blissful dreams of the long months that heralded the coming of each babe has to be paid for now—paid for in pain and unnameable fear. You may know all about this in England, unless you move and meet the storm while it is yet afar from your gates, for that which has happened here will happen to you, not in your children's time, but *now* in your time, for the Goths are out on the war-path, and the maddest devil since Nero has donned his war-paint.

The Glory of Killing Children

William the accursed is hacking his way to power, and his airships are dropping bombs that are blowing women and children to fragments. What does *he* care how many babes he kills—is he not William the anointed of God? What does *he* care how many women's hearts he breaks—he, the mad devil, the spawn of Satan, thinks only of *his* glory?

Think of it—the glory that comes to a man from the mangled bodies of little children. Ye Gods in heaven! it is awful. I have seen the semi-savages in South American States at war—part Indian, part Negro, part Spanish—and I thought I knew how low a country could sink; but it takes a *Kaiser*, a Hohenzollern—the exalted personality in whom German "culture" is focussed—to show to what depths of baseness, love of power and criminal vanity can bring a man and a nation.

The Red Hand of the *Kaiser*

I used to love the Germans. I thought them a grand people, full of high ideals. I know them now. They slay little children and—women. I had not thought to live to see this day—a splendid people led into infamy by a mad dog who has grown blind looking upon himself until he counts himself a god—and such a god! His hand is red with murder, not with war.

The night has passed—the day wears on—the city hums with life. The sky is blue, the meadows near the city blush with beauty. Nature murmurs joyously and the world is glad. It does not seem that even a *Kaiser* can blast all joy out of existence. Devil that he is, his lust of power has limitations. The chime bells peal out joyously to God— only the mothers are white-lipped and heavy-eyed as they watch their broods at play. They do not reason, they do not think. They only *know*.

How do they know, these women? Why do their breasts ache where the sweet lips clung? What instinct is it that makes them weary with anguish they cannot explain? The fathers are brave and strong and steadfast; they do not want to fight but they will fight, and the women know it.

The women stand at their doors chatting. They begin to laugh; the terrors of the time have passed them by. They joke with one another, and sly words pass between old friends conveying things that women tell only to women—a sentence half spoken is checked by a nod, a glance, a touch of a finger on arm or shoulder, a shy look, a downward drooping of the eyes, a little laugh, a matronly blush, a whispered word of hope and cheer heralding the coming of good times when peace shall reign in the land, and then—a blinding flash of intense light, a noise as if hell were growling; doors cave in, ceilings come down, chimneys topple over on roofs, windows crash and smash and clatter, roadways and pavements are torn up; smoke, flame, and fire burst up, the stink of blood and burning flesh, the sudden awful shriek of mangled human beings fill the air and herald the greatness, the grandeur, the manly magnificence of the *Kaiser*.

When the Smoke has Cleared Away

The Zeppelin floats away. It sails high above the town; so high it seems only a speck in the blue where God is supposed to be watching and smiling at this holocaust of those who dared to frown on him whom God had made *Kaiser* of the Germans and ruler of millions

FREAKISH EFFECT OF A
ZEPPELIN BOMB EXPLOSION
ON A PARISIAN DWELLING.
ON THE LEFT IS A HOUSE, SIX
OF WHOSE FLOORS ARE
COMPLETELY SECTIONED BY
AN INFERNAL MACHINE

—according to the cult of the great parricide.

The smoke clears away, the Zeppelin has gone far out of reach, the splendid warriors who dropped the bombs have scurried off to tell to William's delighted ears the news of the work so bravely done, and in the roadway lie the fruits of German chivalry, the aftermath of Teuton bravery—a woman who gave suck to a babe at the breast, and some little children mangled, ripped and torn and twisted, dying from hurt.

And this is kingcraft; this the ripe fruit of all that high philosophy, which savants have acclaimed for a generation past; this is Germany at her best and highest—a war on pregnant women and toddling babes, on old grey men and peaceful *burghers*—why? To fill the accursed boast that never has a Hohenzollern lived and reigned who did not add some miles of stolen territory to Germanic powers.

Triumph of the Aeroplane in the War

By Claude Grahame-White and Harry Harper

Military aeroplanes were, at the outbreak of the Great War, efficient in two only of the five uses tor which they are destined in future warfare. They were able, firstly, to act as scouts; and, secondly, to direct the fire of artillery; but there were no fighting, armoured aeroplanes worthy of the name, and no machines suitable for attacking successfully a strongly-fortified position, nor were there aircraft capable of the rapid transport of troops. From the point of view of a perfected aeroplane—of machines which should carry out all these tasks—the war came five years too soon.

The scouting aeroplane, on which designers had concentrated their attention, was the most practical of flying craft. It braved wind and fog, rain, and even snow, and ran the gauntlet of hostile gun fire. From the severest test, under most arduous conditions, it emerged triumphant.

It is possible for an aviator, using a highspeed machine, to reach an enemy's position that is three days' march away, observe the disposition of his forces, and then return to headquarters—all within a space of three hours. More than once, when rapidity in scouting was essential, the aeroplane performed work of supreme importance.

THE AEROPLANE'S IMMENSE VALUE IN RECONNAISSANCE

The best instance occurred at Mons. Sir John French, hearing from General Joffre on the evening of August 23rd that the British position was threatened by three German army corps on its front, with another seeking to turn its flank, needed to confirm this news before dark, so that he might decide what should be done next day at dawn. Considerable distances had to be traversed in such a reconnaissance, and only an hour or so of daylight remained.

No other instrument of war could, in the time, have done what the British aircraft did. A number of them flew out, each following a specified route, and in an hour, thanks to their speed and to the fact that no land obstructions caused them deviation or delay, they had collected news which it might have taken cavalry scouts a day to glean. The enemy were seen, their strength estimated; "the fog of war" was pierced and swept aside. And that night, in his headquarters, making ready for the coming day, Sir John French was able to plan the fighting retreat.

Aircraft enables a commander-in-chief to see, as Wellington always longed to see, what is occurring "on the other side of the hill." War ceases to be haphazard, with those who control it making fumbling moves, vaguely aware only of what an adversary is doing. As Major-General Henderson has said:

> Throughout a campaign, where both sides are sufficiently equipped with aircraft, the game must be played with the cards on the table.

Secrecy in operations, the striking of an unseen blow, becomes enormously difficult now there are these scouts in the air. And for this reason, as the war has shown, the use of aircraft has had a marked influence on strategy. It has rendered extraordinarily important the factors of time and distance.

A commander-in-chief, if he hopes for success, must try to adapt the tactics of Napoleon, the originator of modern war, to these new conditions that prevail. He must aim at his enemy so swift and powerful a blow, at a point where this enemy's line is weakest, and least able to call up support, that even if the stroke is seen by the air scouts before it is struck, it possesses such rapidity, such irresistible force, that it will succeed in the face of detection.

Mathematics for Anti-Aircraft Gunners

Anti-aircraft artillery, semi-automatic in its action and throwing shells to a height greater than that at which an aviator will fly if he is to do practical work as a scout, has been used vigorously against the aeroplane. But the latter, thanks to its speed and manoeuvring power and to the small target it offers, has rarely been hit, and its work is impeded by gun fire to no serious extent.

Flight-Com. Grahame-White chats with a British
soldier and French airman in France.

One of the fastest single-seated scouts, when at its highest speed, will travel more than one hundred and seventy feet in a second; and as a shell may take two or three seconds to rise to the altitude at which a machine is flying, this means that, between the moment at which the gun is fired and the bursting of the shell at the height for which it is timed, the aeroplane that is the target may have travelled several hundred feet.

This entails for the gunner an intricate calculation in which, basing his aim on an estimate of the speed of the aircraft, he points his weapon at the moment of discharge at some point in the air which may be eight or ten lengths in advance of the machine. And there is, in addition to calculating the speed of the aeroplane, the difficulty of estimating its height, which will change constantly as the pilot manoeuvres his machine. It is not surprising, therefore, that while many aircraft run this gauntlet of fire, few are brought to the ground.

Aeroplane as Range-finder for Artillery

In directing long-range artillery, which may be bombarding some position its gunners cannot see, the aeroplane succeeded beyond all hope. A pilot ascends, watched by the officers of the battery with which he is co-operating. He flies over the enemy, observing their positions. When he sees concealed trenches or hidden guns, which it would be impossible to detect save from his bird's-eye view, he drops a smoke-bomb, which marks the spot, whereupon the officers who are watching his flight, working out the range by means of a telemeter or some other sighting instrument, proceed to drop their shells just over the area that has been indicated.

In one instance, which shows the accuracy that can be obtained, an aviator was passing above a village in the enemy's territory when he observed in the garden of a lonely cottage a gathering of figures, which, having regard to the military motorcars he saw drawn up nearby, suggested to him that this might be a meeting of the Headquarters Staff.

Such, indeed, it was. The airman dropped his marking bomb. It was seen through their field-glasses by the artillery officers for whom he was range-finding, and who were lying among some bushes on a hilltop three miles away.

Of course, they could not see what the airman saw. They had to take it for granted that what he had observed below was worth expending ammunition upon. The range was worked out, and one of the guns which was standing on the hillside just below them, shielded by a screen of bushes, was trained so as to throw a shell at this target that was invisible. The gun roared, and the shell sped away with a whine that rose quickly to a shriek.

Accurate Aim at Unseen Target

Those in the garden of the cottage heard the shell coming towards them, rending the air with its harsh, grim note. It took them by surprise, because no bombardment was in progress in this corner of the battlefield. But there was no time to move to safety; there was, in fact, no shelter for which to run.

The frail cottage, were it struck, would prove a death-trap. So, the generals and their staff stood silent by the map-strewn table, waiting the arrival of this messenger of death. The shell swept down at them, struck, and burst; the earth splashed up in a fountain, and there arose an inky, sluggish cloud of smoke.

But instead of landing in the garden, as it should have done, the shell dropped twenty-five yards too short. It tore a gap through the garden hedge, and dug a pit on the other side, besides covering the officers and their maps with a fine spray of mould. But for this trifling error of yards, they were devoutly thankful; it was just enough to save their lives. Such shooting is wonderful, none the less. Remember that the gunners who fired could obtain no glimpse of their target. Yet at a distance of three miles, and at their first shot, they were so near their unseen target that they sprinkled it with earth by the bursting of their shell.

Of fighting aeroplanes, when the war began, there were a few craft which had been fitted with machine-guns; but these were experimental and slow-flying, and had technical defects. Yet there was aerial fighting, none the less. British and French aviators, triumphing over the limitations of their craft, attacked the German airmen with rifles and revolvers, making up in personal gallantry what they lacked in armament.

Apart from the skill required to bring an adversary to combat in the air and impose your tactics on his, the courage of the airman needs to be exceptional. His machine, as he steers for his foe, is moving through the air at a very high speed; and to handle this craft, apart from any question of manoeuvring for a conflict, requires much dexterity.

Rapid Manoeuvring and Aerial Conflict

The evolutions of two machines as they draw together in combat are so rapid that an observer from the ground can scarcely follow them. The positions of the antagonists change constantly in regard to each other. A pilot is above his enemy's head one moment, then suddenly he may dive below him, and the next instant, by a turn at a critical moment, he may avoid a conflict and dart away. The difficulty of accurate firing is extreme. From a machine passing through the air at eighty or a hundred miles an hour the marksman has to aim at another craft which is also in rapid flight, and follows no given course or altitude, but is altering its position ceaselessly both as regards elevation and range. And in the airman's brain, though it may be sub-conscious, lies the thought that a shot from his enemy, if it strikes him or hits a vital part of his machine, may send him earthward in a fall which spells death, and from which there is no escape.

The bold tactics of the allied airmen, who forced a combat whenever possible, had a distinctly weakening effect on the German initiative. But, remembering this, and granting also the use, as the war progressed, of a more perfect type of gun-carrying craft, there was no chance of so interfering with the enemy that he lost the services of his flying scouts. It is the keynote of aerial strategy that, immediately war is declared, you should seek to bring your foe to combat, and so cripple him that, in subsequent stages of the campaign, his flying scouts may be beaten back when they attempt to penetrate your lines and observe your dispositions.

In this way, while blindfolding your enemy, you are still able to see yourself. Your adversary will fight, so to say, in twilight, while you are in the light of day. But in this campaign, owing to a lack of machines, and through the inadequacy of weapons, none of the contending air corps have been able to inflict a crushing blow, and the result has been that both by the Germans and the Allies a constant use of aircraft has been possible.

Human Element and the Mechanical

Surprising results were obtained during the war by the use of aeroplanes in destructive raids. Airship stations were attacked with conspicuous success; they offered large and vulnerable targets. Ammunition and supply depots were raided with great effect; while in attacks on troops in bivouac, or on the march, which should be judged more by their demoralising influence than by the actual damage done, airmen harassed the enemy and prevented him from resting, even when in camps behind the battle-front.

But here again the triumph of the air corps was more human than mechanical. By flying low and risking their lives every second, as did

British naval airmen at Düsseldorf and Cuxhaven, the bomb-droppers managed to hit the targets at which they aimed. Only in this way— by descending deliberately into the danger-zone, and launching their missiles from heights of a few hundred feet—could they have overcome the difficulties that exist in dropping bombs with accuracy from an aeroplane in flight.

But the aerial history of the war, when it is written, will show that it is as scouts and as range-finders for artillery that the flying corps did their really vital work.

The Fight of the Flaming Ship

By Max Pemberton

On the borders of Lake Constance was the ship born, and there upon her they made the sign of the Iron Cross.

A great occasion for the Hun, and celebrated with Hunnish joviality. Fat men were there whose breasts jangled orders; lean men pressed in and out of the crowd and piped their feeble voices. The deuce and all was played with the sausages. Not only must the gasbag be filled, but also the balloons of culture. Looking ahead, the bespangled fire-eaters declared that England was finished. The Zeppelin stood in the heaven and all was well with the world below.

Later on, the ship is in another place. It is the same ship but different. The idea that drifted over Lake Constance half a decade ago has become the fact which a hangar in Flanders or the islands shall shelter. It is a wonderful sight, and guarded by sentries most vigilant. Puny man looks up at it from below and stands aghast at its immensity.

The child upon a wharf does not regard the sheer sides of a monster liner with greater veneration—yet how different are these twain! The one will house three thousand people. It is an hotel, and again an hotel. Its engine-room is like a church; its crew alone may number a thousand souls.

Not so the Zeppelin. But twenty-eight or thirty will manoeuvre this vastness. Here are neither bathrooms nor lifts, restaurants nor bridge-saloons. The cabins are but enlarged canoes. Men go hazardously with muffled feet upon a single plank. You could not whip a cat in the engine-room. The captain sits apart like the driver of a car in the Tube, his switchboard before him, his instruments ready to his hand. But the seat of his authority is small. The landsman peeps in his cabin with awe and shivers, maybe, when he contemplates his responsibility.

117

BRITISH NAVAL AVIATOR RESCUED BY SUBMARINE AFTER THE
CHRISTMAS AIR-RAID ON CUXHAVEN

On Murder Bent

Look at the crew—volunteers all, and paid high wages. Years ago, when the motorcar was a new thing upon an English high road, we saw strange animals within them, and perchance the populace jeered. "'Twas not alone the inky cloak, good mother." Men wrapped themselves in many thicknesses, and coat was laid upon coat—fur over all and leather in between. There were hooded varieties, and they were not labelled. The intensity of the cold put Arctic boots even upon the feet of dilettante wanderers. Some such hybrids are the crew of the Zepp. Fur and flannel go to their making. Their boots are felt with a lining of fur. They have the cabbage ears and slit eyes of the Oriental. "Sportsmen," you say but that is wholly too generous. They have courage, but are without pity. Well they know the object for which the Colossus was built. "*Gott strafe* England!" is on their lips as they climb the ladders to the cabins which enshroud them. There will be dead women and children in London tomorrow. God save the *Kaiser*!

The Dream of Daedalus

It is the truth. And yet, Heaven knows the whole thing would be romantic enough if these were the piping times. Here is the dream of Daedalus, and as this dream shall fall, so fell less terribly Icarus, the son. Fifteen hundred years have not changed man at all. Jules Verne put him in a balloon and sent him across Africa. The small boy of a hundred generations had longed for that. To leave the world behind, to make faces at your enemy from a height, to tempt the lion with a sawdust ham and then to run helter-skelter for your ladder and your balloon—what joy!

Zeppelin the Terrible made it all possible. Given petrol and oil, you could cross Africa easily enough today, as Jules Verne crossed it—is it not forty years ago? But the peace of it was never in the destroyer's mind. The hope of slaughter and champagne went hand in hand on the feast day; and slaughter alone without the champagne now sends the Zepp. from its hangar across the North Sea to the hated shores. Meteorologists all over the place have said that the barometric conditions are favourable; there will be no dreaded north-easter tonight. The moon, as the old song has it, is behind a tree. A little wraith of mist will smoke about the dragon, and its teeth will be hidden awhile. But there will be no storm and so—let her rip! The men have fed well, and their wool is buttoned close around them. Militarism permits of

119

no cuddled farewells. They climb to their seats, and the captain, with a last look round, takes his place at the wheel. Let her go now! It is day, and the children who will be dead tonight are laughing in the sun.

It is a fair journey, and if it be from the north, will show you something of Holland, perchance, and the fat Dutchmen below. A dull old dog he is, yet with wit enough to fire a gun if fingers be too loudly snapped in his jovial face. The North Sea itself is but a grey waste beyond the coast, and the ships upon it are few. In a more frolicsome mood this grim Hun at the wheel would toss bombs upon them for luck and wish them "God-speed!" But today he has other work to do.

CRYING FOR THE DARK

Should he have come, not from the north but from the great hangars by Bruges, he will cross our old friend Zeebrugge, and look down upon the batteries which once were golf-links as fine as any in Flanders. They will cheer him there, and cheers are music in ears grown deaf to curses. From a height, it may be, of 5,000 feet at this point, he will see Ostend, white and shining in the curve of the bay, and broken Nieuport beyond it, and La Panne upon the coast, and the desolation of the waters by which Belgium drove his fellows back when the hour was critical.

Perchance, too, he may spy out the dim shape of a British warship like a fleck of black upon a cold grey carpet. But all these are without interest to him upon this afternoon of autumn. Now he is crying for the dark to come down. The shadows gather, and sea and shore alike are blotted from his view.

A shaded lamp shows him the face of his instrument-board, and the buttons with which he will release the bombs presently. He pushes on with a luminous compass for his only guide, and *anon* his bearings trouble him. If London be the goal, he should be somewhere in the neighbourhood of Harwich by this time. He drops a star-shell, and lo and behold! its blinding blue light turns to a cold whiteness, which reveals the mouth of a great river and ships at anchor, and below the Zepp. the houses of a village and the curves of a bay. "It is Felixstowe," says the Hun, and instantly correcting his helm, he hurries on for London—and death.

A HORRIBLE ALTERNATIVE

He is at a great altitude now. Every effort of his twin engines was needed to lift the weight of bombs as he drew near the white cliffs; and he seeks the shelter of any cloud as though a friendly hand were outstretched to him. The country immediately beyond the cliffs has little interest for him. Here and there a faint shimmer of light will speak of town or village. A deeper glow tells of a railway or shipping in the river. London itself cannot be perceived until the rim of it is crossed.

But the clock and the speedometer will tell the fellow where he is, and the river will guide him infallibly. For all that, this is no gay pilgrimage.

These marauders go with no laugh upon their lips. The dullest imagination can but speculate upon the "might be." Down and yet down through the darkness, flung like a stone from the sky, brought up at last with a dreadful crash beyond which is night and blackness that is the mildest penalty of disaster. There is an alternative so horrible that men must clench their hands when they think of it. If this great balloon above them were fired! The terror of it is beyond comprehension. They put it from their thoughts, and lick their lips because the prey is at hand. Surely this England whom they would strafe is asleep. But is she?

In a great garage "somewhere in the silver isle" there has been a note of alarm tonight. Peep into the place and you will see strange doings. Yonder are the sheds, but they are lighted and their doors are open. Before them upon the grass are the hornets whom the winter night will set buzzing. Their wings are already spread and they have eaten.

Oddly clad men move about them and test their pennons with tender fingers. There is work to be done, and it requires courage like to none that war has yet called for. The good fellows look above to the blackness of the clouded sky, and tell themselves that the enemy is there.

Anon the word to go is given. One by one the engines are started with a roar and a rattle. The hornets spread their wings and skim away and disappear in the darkness. They circle and rise. They are cut off from all things living. The lights of the great city become but a glow beneath them. They, too are thinking of women and children. God, what work to do!

EXCITEMENT OF THE ADVENTURE

And so back to the Zepp. The Hun has not liked it overmuch since he left that fair town of Harwich, and, in truth, his heart has been more than once in his mouth. Objectionable people, swinging the shoulder-pieces of guns deftly, have used the goniometric range-finder, of which he thinks so much, and have peppered him with shrapnel most "demnibly." Profiting by his own instruction books, they have described the sky parallelogram and filled it cheerfully with messages of goodwill. Bullets sing about the monster and the air cracks with detonations. More than once the chief Hun thought that he was hit, and put feverish questions to the crew.

But this, after all, is the peril with which habit has made him familiar, and he is willing to take his chances. At the worst he can bring the great ship down and take a rest cure at Donington. It is of that greater danger he will not think until he must. London is now ahead of him, and he circles about it for the objective which he will call military. Shrapnel still follows him, but the excitement of the adventure prevails above the dread of it. He touches a trigger and a bomb falls upon the awakened city. Plainly to the raiders' ears comes the boom of that resounding explosion. Perchance those who were alive ten seconds ago are dead this instant. The crew chortles in its joy—another and another! Doing well tonight, and undiscovered by those cursed searchlights. A vain boast.

The words are hardly spoken when the great silver beam wings up from the blackness below, and the ship is shown as a fairy in a limelight. No more bombing now, be sure of it. Every nerve must be strained, every trick be tried to escape this damning publicity. See how the gigantic snake is wriggling? Here and there, to the right, to the left, up and down—a rat seeking a hole is not in a greater hurry. For well these fellows know what that revelation means. Already the omens are buzzing in their ears. "A 'plane!" cry twenty voices. Figures cower and huddle in the depths of the cabin. Is this the end?

The aviator is alone, and all the living world he has known seems far away. Of his own peril he has no sense. He is cut off from the earth, and in this vast blackness of the ether he sees but one objective. The great path of silver light links earth and sky; but it shows him the gate of the seventh heaven. If only he can do it! What joy to the millions awake and awaiting there in the city which has sent him forth! His gun is ready and the "jolly"-stick is between his legs now. He can give but an occasional hand to it, and that for the swift manoeuvre. Clearly, he sees the very faces of the Huns. There is the sharp rattle of discharge, but no answer from the monster.

BEGINNING OF THE END

He climbs above it with tremendous acceleration of his willing engine, and again he presses his shoulder to the piece. If he can but do it! His new discharge has helped him no better than the old. He hardly

Zeppelins are capable of carrying, in addition to their crews, bombs weighing in the aggregate about a ton and a half. The chief menace to a Zeppelin is attack by aeroplanes, which are much swifter and capable of rising much higher. They can circle round a Zeppelin and drop bombs on it. So Zeppelins are frequently mounted with guns of high-angle range to repel attacking aeroplanes. To discharge such a gun is fraught with danger to the Zeppelin, but that danger must be faced

HOW A ZEPPELIN FIGHTS ATTACK FROM ABOVE

realises at this time that he is in an aeroplane at all. A mad excitement possesses him. In all that vastness of infinity there is but one star and he must win it. Down he goes and round, the answering bullets singing about him, the roar of the enemy's gun now loud in his ears. A new manoeuvre has sent him winging to the rear of Colossus, and putting in his last belt he prays to God that he may get her. Now a sharp rattle follows the speeding of the bullet. He swerves and comes upon a new tack—and so he sees, and who shall find words for him?

It all began with a little glow of rosy red light at the rear of the tremendous envelope. The light spreads. It is as the coming of the sun upon a lone mountain peak—at first but a pink flush, *anon* a flame, and then the whole glory of the day. So here shall be the glory of the night. See, now the envelope has burst and with a mighty roar the flame has rushed about it. The doomed men in the cars below, listening to the sounds, utter one doleful, piercing cry when the truth is understood.

In the Furnace of Destiny

An instant later and they are themselves enveloped in that furnace of their destiny. So awful are their cries that the man in the aeroplane wings away for very terror of them. Here and there one, unable to suffer the agony, leaps from the car and crashes over headlong to the black earth beneath. The rest have become but shrivelled trunks, dying helplessly, it may be without consciousness of time or place.

But the Zepp. itself is now a flaring beacon for all the countryside. Men will tell their children in the years to come that they saw it fifty miles from London town. Great crowds throng the streets and point at it. There are those who weep for very joy. But, in the main, it is a glad cry upon the falling. Cheer oh, and again cheer oh! Read by this splendid lamp the story of the salvation of woman and child The Zepp. is down, and the man who took her is up yonder somewhere in the flaring heavens—alone—and it may be that, now, he also is afraid.

Triumph of the Air Force in the Battle for Amiens

By Edward Wright

Until the spring of 1918 the air forces of the Western Allies lacked the power to show the possibilities of an aerial offensive. Surprised by the Fokker scourge in 1916 and temporarily mastered by the Albatros peril of 1917, British and French aviators had as much as they could do to carry on with the inferior machines generally provided them Strangely long it took both the British and French Governments to

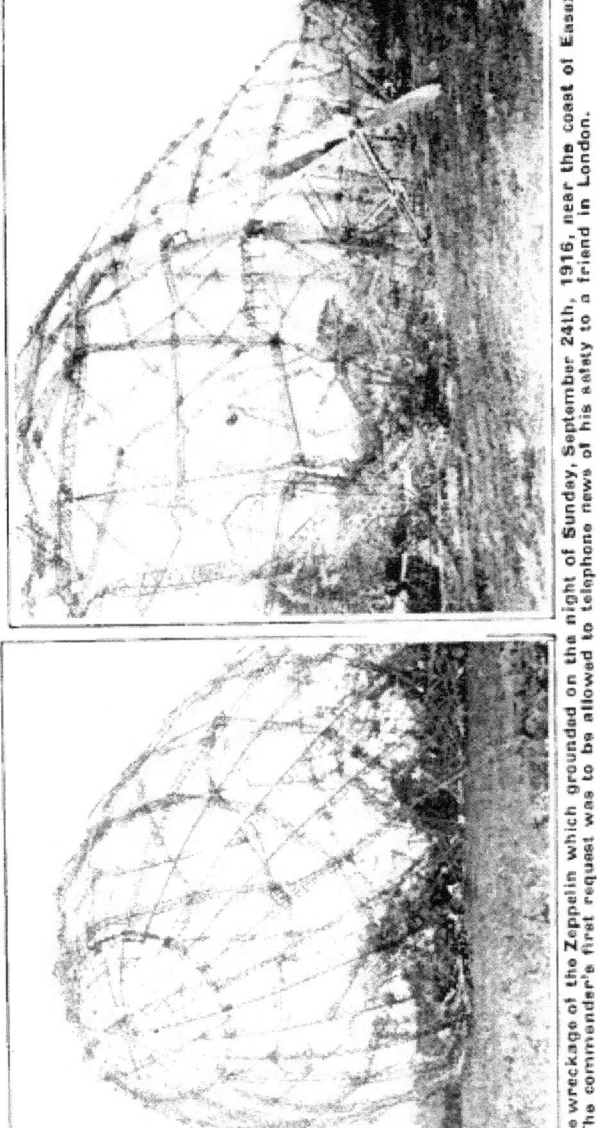

Two views of the wreckage of the Zeppelin which grounded on the night of Sunday, September 24th, 1916, near the coast of Essex. The commander's first request was to be allowed to telephone news of his safety to a friend in London.

produce directors of aircraft supplies with sufficient managing ability and foresight to organise all the manufacturing resources of the two countries. This, however, was at last done, with the result that the enemy was in turn surprised and mastered by the superior productiveness of allied aeroplane works. All he could do in the way of preparation he did, but with the lull combined talents of Britain and France against him he was clean excelled alike in quantity and quality.

General von Ludendorff was aware of this situation when he opened his grand offensive on March 21st, 1918. His position was somewhat similar to that of Sir John Jellicoe immediately before the Battle of Jutland Bank. The British admiral could not fight in clear weather, because his movements would have been foreseen by hostile naval airships. He therefore selected a day of dense, low-lying cloud for his great sweep into the Skager Rack, so that Zeppelins should not be able to operate against him.

LIFTING OF THE FOG

General von Ludendorff chose a day of thick mist, in which British aeroplanes could not work; and, with little help from his own air forces, his enormous number of concentrated divisions broke through the Fifth British Army, turned the right flank of the Third British Army, and, crowding into the large angle between the Somme and Oise Rivers, menaced both Paris and Abbeville, the point at which the British and French forces could be divided. The misty weather continued for about fifty critical hours, completing the confusion of the divided and overwhelmed forces of defence, by making it impossible for their contact machines to watch over brigades, trace battalions, or scout for lost companies.

When on March 23rd the fog of disaster lifted, the alert, well-ordered armies of Marwitz and Hutier were the first to profit by the clearing of the sky. Their aerodromes were undisturbed, their machines and pilots ready and eager; so that the tired, hungry, yet dogged British soldiers, trying to form a defensive flank about Péronne, often saw three huge enemy formations holding the air above them and not a British machine in sight.

This absence from the battlefield of British machines seemed the crowning misery of the great disaster. Yet it was really the saving of the general situation. British pilots were massing in another and unexpected direction for something more important than rearguard observation. All the Western Allies were then arranging the largest and swiftest concentration of air-power hitherto seen in the war. General Pétain, who had massed his main armies in Champagne, in answer to a deceptive demonstration by Gallwitz, could not move horse, foot, and guns quickly enough to fill the gap left by the overwhelmed Britons. He had thought that the Oise River line, between Moy and La Fère, would be unbreakable at the time it was breaking.

But the man who had saved Verdun by hurrying up three thousand motor-lorries was not at the end of his resources. He could not get cavalry or infantry forward, but he stripped his front of crack pilots on chaser 'planes and experienced bombers on the larger machines Then, as soon as possible, a United States aerial detachment also left the Lorraine front for the Oise and Somme battlefield.

Aerial Counter-Offensive

The main air force of Great Britain was already working over the scene of the disastrous retreat, and from reports of its numerous scouts the plan of a novel and extraordinary aerial counter-offensive was framed and put into execution.

What then happened cannot fully be described. Nobody immediately concerned in it caught anything more than glimpses of a prolonged air struggle lasting a month. The clash of aerial fleets was quite different in character from the sharp, clear-cut action of naval forces. It was a tangled affair of airy skirmishes, swooping raids and bombing expeditions upon supply trains. Some of the most picturesque incidents were of least importance, while seemingly dull, sordid work—such as dropping explosives upon mules and horses, and then raking the poor beasts with machine-gun fire—proved events of high strategic value.

Beneath the united air forces of the Allies were at first a broken British Army, fragments of which were merging into a small French reinforcement of *Chasseurs a pied*, with cavalry and armoured motor detachments. They were so thinly scattered as to give no large targets to enemy aviators. The German Army, on the other hand, was in immense multitudes, limited only by the number of roads and byways down which supply columns could crawl. From the point of view of the counter-attacking forces of allied airmen the conditions of battle were wonderfully promising; and, neglecting for a while the secondary task of protecting the British infantry rear-guards from swooping German machines, the British air commander boldly and decisively carried the surprising counteroffensive far back into the enemy's original lines.

TONING–UP AN IMMENSE R.A.F. MACHINE
DEPARTING ON BOMBING RAID INTO GERMANY.

"Blockaded" from the Air

First in scores and then in hundreds, British and French bombing machines attacked the piled and crowded railheads from which General von Hutier's army was working. By day the roads and narrow-gauge tracks feeding his advancing divisions were swept with aerial machine-gun fire and bombed with small missiles. When night fell, and the traffic of the enemy increased to the uttermost, until all the ways of movement were densely packed with men, mules, horses, waggons, lorries, tractors, and guns, bombing operations grew in scope and intensity, until air-power was at last seen to be superior to land-power.

Mastery in the air was not displayed in the manner prophesied by some writers. The forty-two enemy infantry divisions, with their thousands of guns, were not bombed or machine-gunned to a standstill. They were blockaded. For example, the apparently overwhelming force that tried to break from Albert and Bray and, turning again the right flank of the Third Army, sweep along to Abbeville by the northern bank of the Somme, was cut off from its supplies by an incessant rain of destruction upon its communications. The Bapaume road became such a death-trap that everything German had at last to avoid it.

It was the aerial attack upon the German new and old communications—thirty miles and more deep in places—that decided the course of the first battle for Amiens. The commander of the enemy flying corps was outmanoeuvred by General J. M. Salmond. The German general merely imitated the aerial cavalry pursuit tactics invented by Sir Hugh Trenchard at Ypres in the autumn of 1917, but while his pilots were wasting time and power attacking small scattered bodies of British infantry, an extraordinary blow was delivered against the stomach of the German Army.

Turning the Tide of Battle

Both food and ammunition were stopped from reaching the hostile advanced forces. In some important cases the movements of fresh reinforcing divisions were impeded and confused. By the time the German air commander saw his mistake, and reconcentrated his squadrons for the vital defence of communications, the tide of battle had been definitely turned from the air. The German pilots were as completely overwhelmed as the infantry of the Fifth British Army had been. In the course of two months' fighting British aviators brought down the remarkable number of one thousand enemy machines, and dropped the equally remarkable quantity of one thousand tons of bombs upon enemy depots, dumps, traffic, and marching columns.

In addition, there were days in which a quarter of a million rounds of machine-gun fire were poured, by British machines alone, upon German troops and vehicles. The achievement of the French aviation service was almost as great, and the work of the United States squadrons counted in the decisive result.

Under the desperate stimulus of a grave disaster a grand new method of warfare had been invented. As Germany was reduced to a position of marked enfeeblement in the air, the new allied technique of an aerial blockade of hostile ways of supply seemed to promise more than any modern naval blockade could attain. In classic Greek sculpture the spirit of victory was represented with wings. And over the field of defeat a winged victory still hovered while Great Britain was gathering new strength for the final struggle.

The Doom of the Aerial Armada

By Max Pemberton

There was no Francis Drake playing bowls upon Plymouth Hoe; no beating of drums to call the yeomen out; no beacons upon headland, height, or ness—just a dark and gloomy night of October, 1917, with a loom of mist above and a glimmer of light below. Yet London knew at an early hour that the Armada had sailed, and devoutly she prayed that the fireships were ready.

A great Armada it was we now know—eleven or thirteen, the estimates still vary—of the monster frigates of the line which were to lay London in ruins. From far Schleswig they came and the bowels of the islands—from Wilhelmshaven and the Kiel district. And they rose majestically. The Angel of Death was abroad, and you could hear the beating of his wings.

Meanwhile London, knowing little of the true circumstances, took the thing very calmly. The streets still numbered their pedestrians; the theatres were full; the omnibuses continued to run. The captains and the kings of the soaring hosts meant nothing to them. An hour had passed, and another, and for all we knew the bowls might yet be rolling.

When the aerial torpedo at length fell, it was a very bolt from the blue. Men gazed into the gloom as though some devilish miracle had been worked. The police picked up the dead. All who could hurried into shelter, asking what next. How little they knew of the tragedy which had run its first act—up there, miles above the earth.

Master Boreas makes His Bow

There were many ships in the Armada, and in pride they had gone forth. No Drake had England, they might have said; but that was a lie. for there were thousands of him in our Air Service, and no bowls were these foemen playing. Brave as they were and ready for the combat, even they had as yet no idea of the lusty old dog who was to give them a hand upon an occasion so memorable. Master Boreas, long forgotten, put on sock and buskin and made his bow. He would play an old part, and we might keep our fireships in port. It is even possible that this worthy old gentleman so far forgot himself as to say "be d———d to them!" It is quite certain that he was one of the first in the field, and that had we, on the pavements below, been aware of his agility, we should have given him a round of applause which any great actor might have envied.

Indeed, it was a turn of fortune most wonderful to record. The monster ships, rising proudly from Hun soil, soaring as gigantic birds of the night, found themselves in a North Sea mist of which no compass could make anything. They sought to rise above it, but the north wind took them. And now, we may suppose, some glimmer of the truth dawned upon them.

Down there, far beneath that bank of freezing mists, was the England they had come to terrify. The cloud was riven for an instant, and a vomit of flame came forth. About them their best ears could detect the hum of aeroplane engines, and they knew that Drake had sailed. Soon the chill of terror is to follow upon that of doubt. The frost is intense, and their own engines begin to fail. It must have come to them as one of their own bolts from the blue that this Armada was surely doomed.

The Beginning of the End

So, we see them drifting helplessly. Many a gun has been fired at them while they crossed the coast many a gallant fellow in a British fireship has come like a bat in the night to tear their long hair with his claws. Their own situation is tragic. They know not where they are; see nothing but the billowed mists which rage and toss about them; hear little but the moaning voice of the terrible winds. Truly are they drifting away from known things to the ethereal caves of spirits and of devils. In their desperation they heave their bombs headlong; fire their torpedoes, they know not at what. Far below they hear the echo of explosions, and then the silence falls again, and the voice of the wind

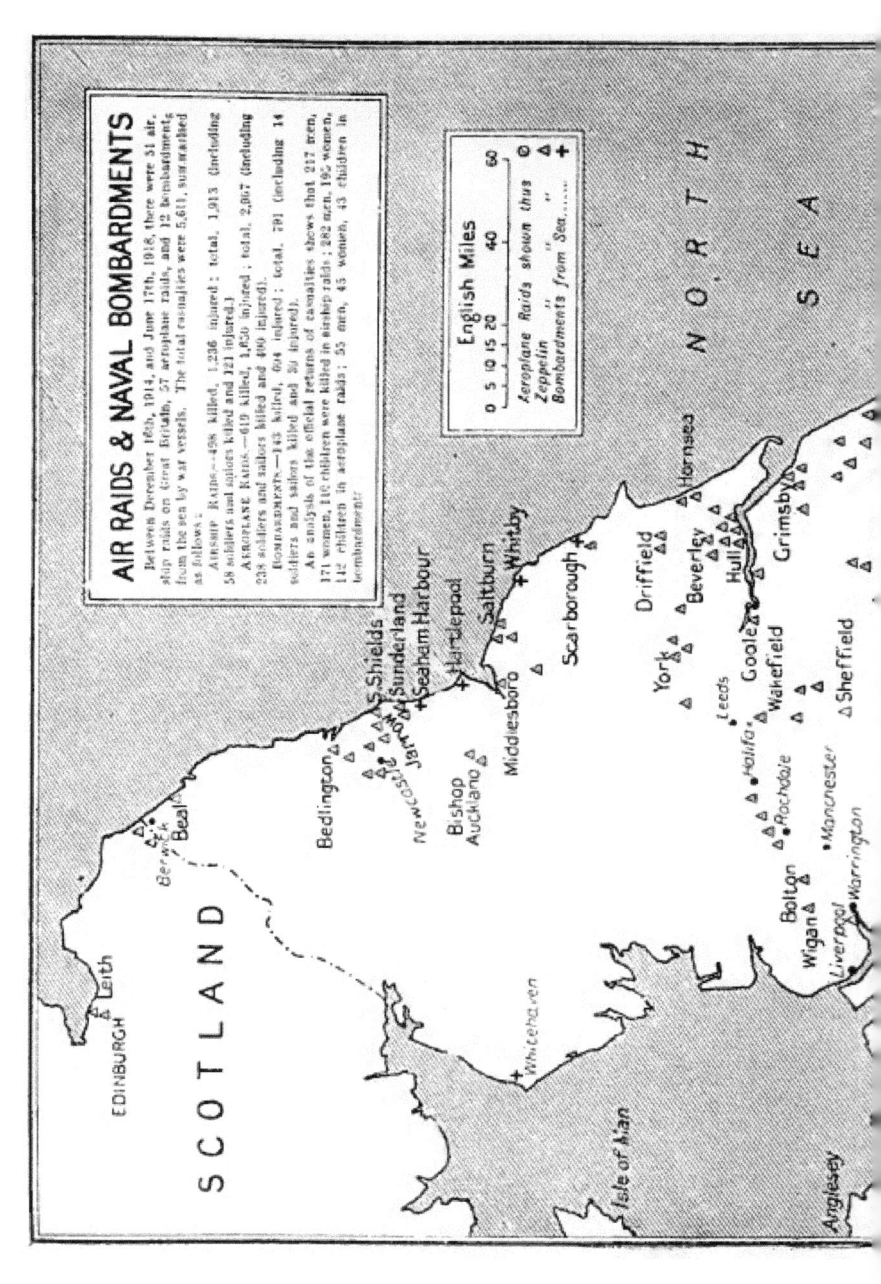

AIR RAIDS & NAVAL BOMBARDMENTS

Between December 16th, 1914, and June 17th, 1918, there were 51 air-ship raids on Great Britain, 57 aeroplane raids, and 12 bombardments from the sea by war vessels. The total casualties were 5,611, summarised as follows:—

AIRSHIP RAIDS.—498 killed, 1,236 injured: total, 1,913 (including 58 soldiers and sailors killed and 121 injured.)

AEROPLANE RAIDS.—619 killed, 1,650 injured: total, 2,067 (including 238 soldiers and sailors killed and 460 injured).

BOMBARDMENTS.—143 killed, 604 injured: total, 791 (including 14 soldiers and sailors killed and 36 injured).

An analysis of the official returns of casualties shows that 217 men, 171 women, 110 children were killed in airship raids; 282 men, 195 women, 142 children in aeroplane raids; 55 men, 45 women, 43 children in bombardments.

English Miles
0 5 10 15 20   40   60

Aeroplane Raids shown thus ...... ◎
Zeppelin   "   "   ...... △
Bombardments from Sea...... +

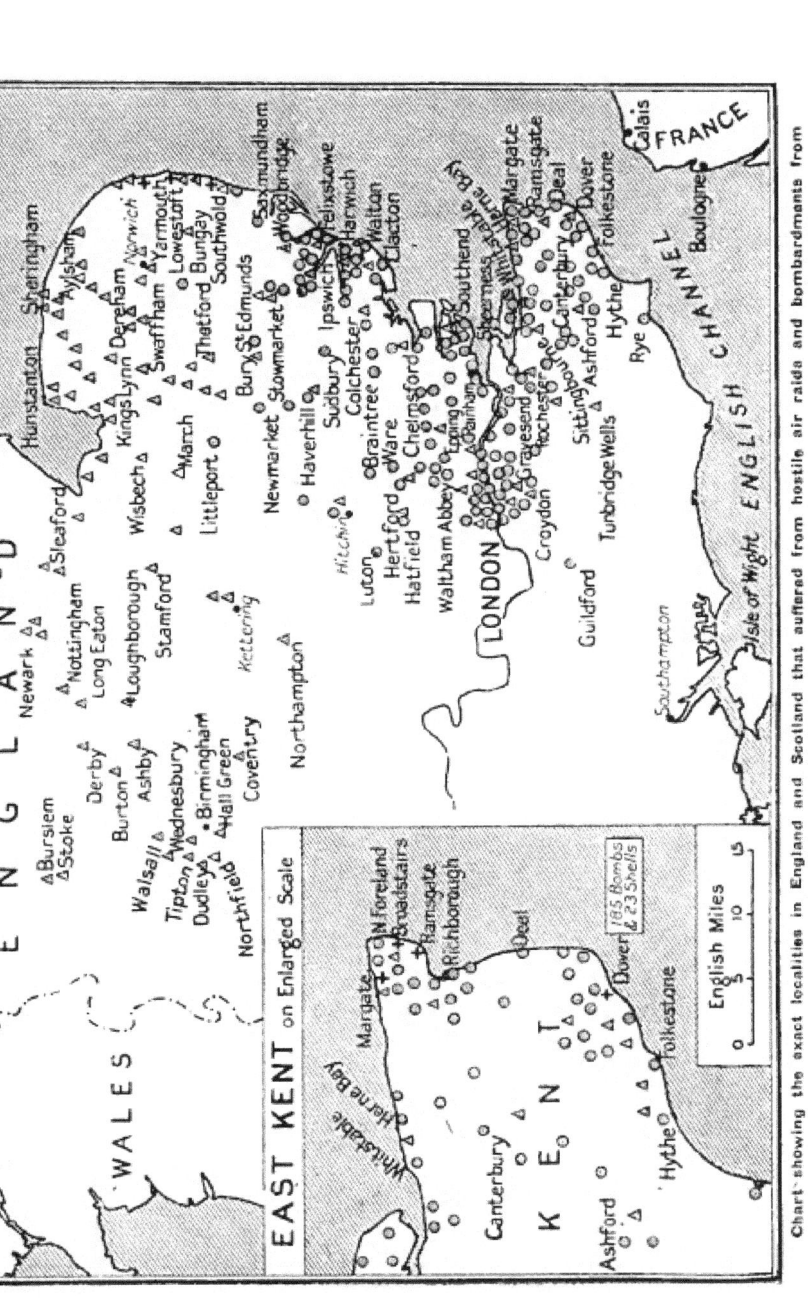

Chart showing the exact localities in England and Scotland that suffered from hostile air raids and bombardments from December 16th, 1914, to June 17th, 1918.

WALES

E N G L A N D

Bursiem
Stoke
Derby
Burton
Walsall
Ashby
Tipton
Wednesbury
Dudley
Birmingham
Hall Green
Northfield
Coventry

Newark
Nottingham
Long Eaton
Loughborough
Stamford
Kettering
Northampton

Sleaford
Wisbech
March
Littleport

Sheringham
Hunstanton
Aylsham
KingsLynn
Swaffham
Dereham
Norwich
Thetford
Bungay
Southwold

Saxmundham
Woodbridge
Felixstowe
Harwich
Walton
Clacton

Newmarket
Stowmarket
Bury St Edmunds
Haverhill
Sudbury
Colchester
Braintree
Ware
Chelmsford

Hitchin
Luton
Hertford
Hatfield
Waltham Abbey
LONDON
Croydon
Guildford

Ipswich
Epping
Rainham
Southend
Sheerness
Canterbury
Gravesend
Rochester
Sittingbourne
Ashford
Hythe
Tunbridge Wells

Aldeburgh
Margate
Ramsgate
Deal
Whitstable
Dover
Folkestone
Rye

Isle of Wight
Southampton

FRANCE
Calais
Boulogne

E N G L I S H   C H A N N E L

EAST KENT on Enlarged Scale

N Foreland
Margate
Broadstairs
Ramsgate
Richborough
Deal

Whitstable
Herne Bay
K   E   N   T
Canterbury
Ashford
Hythe
Folkestone
Dover

185 Bombs & 23 Shells

English Miles
0   5   10   15

alone speaks. There is now no thought of attack, but only of escape, if escape be possible. Their engines run no longer; they are as helpless as wreckage upon a hostile sea—the day can but bring them doom.

At last, it dawns—a wild morning of autumn—and looking down through the breaking clouds the Hun discerns the earth.

What land is this? Is he still above the fair fields of the detested English, or has fate carried him luckily to Belgium and his brethren? Each commander of the eight ships that went drifting thus is soon to learn. It is an odd welcome for brethren to give, for lo! the hornets rise swiftly from the earth, and the machine-guns begin to rattle. There are belching monsters, moreover, which vomit high explosives about *mein herr's* ears, and to him there comes the affrighting thought that this is no land of the Belgians, but fair France herself with her incomparable airmen, her dauntless courage, her matchless gift for all that appertains to aviation. And with what zest she sets about the drifting derelicts! The thrasher upon the back of the whale must be our simile or the hawk that defies the wounded eagle, and drives it headlong to earth at last. Up and at them truly she is, and the daylight has hardly come when the first of the proud ships falls in flames at St. Clement, near Lunéville, and the great last act of the magnificent drama is opened.

How L49 was Captured

To be precise, this was at 6.45 on the morning of Saturday, October 20th. Anti-aircraft guns chiefly seem to have been responsible for the quarry, but at 9.20 a greater triumph was scored when L49 landed at Bourbonne-les-Bains practically intact, and one brave man, armed only with a shot-gun, made the whole of her crew prisoners. No more amazing thing than this was done during the war. Here was M. Jules Boiteux out for a morning stroll, in the hope perchance that he could shoot a partridge for breakfast, when, looking up, he perceives a monstrous gasbag flopping to the earth, and, like one Absalom, much hampered by the branches of a tree. He says:

> The noise of a motor caused me to look up. What was my surprise to see an immense airship surrounded by little French aeroplanes, which were pelting it with machine-guns? The Zeppelin was flying very slowly and extremely low. Suddenly its forepart turned down into a group of trees on a hillock, and the airship remained stationary above the ground. The nineteen men of its crew jumped instantly to the ground. The last of them was the commander, who arranged his men in good

order and gave them their final instructions—then discharged his pistol into the envelope of the balloon.

At this point M. Boiteux thought it was time to take a hand in the proceedings. Up goes his shotgun and the commanders' arms almost at one and the same time. It is "*Kamerad!*" with a vengeance. The brave metallurgical worker, realising in a flash the value to the Allies of this intact ship, took a good aim at the captain of the Huns and plainly intimated what he would do.

Men rushed up to the place, aviators and soldiers raced there, and soon a cordon was formed. They hurried the Boches away, and took possession of the giant ship with all her wonderful instruments unharmed. Shall we wonder that the Hun captain raged and swore, and lifted his impotent hands to heaven? No Zepp had been taken thus since the war began.

Five Accounted For

Now, this was a pretty scene enough, but there was another almost as encouraging to follow. Hardly had our French friends made sure of L49 when L50 appeared, hovered over the scene a little while, but being harassed by aeroplanes made off in the direction of Dammartin. Then, sixteen of her crew climbed down the ladder and said goodbye to the "old 'bus," but she herself rose wearily again, and was no more heard of. No better fortune attended L45, which never seems to have got to England at all, but drifted in the fog along the Valley of the Saone, crossed the Departments of the Isere and the Hautes Alpes, and finally fell at 10.50 a.m. in the bed of a stream called La Buec.

This ship the crew fired, and its end was flame and smoke, as was that of another which was brought down at 4 o'clock on Saturday near Laragne, which is some forty-eight miles S.S.E. of Grenoble. Right across France had these derelicts thus drifted, while of another the story is that it actually passed over Toulon and was last seen hovering over the Mediterranean Sea, into which it may well have fallen. Of the mighty eight, five were thus surely accounted for.

So ended the voyage of the Great Armada. England became "merry" truly at the news. The wild ride of these Valkyries appealed to every imagination, yet its terrors may be imagined by lew. To our own splendid fellows and to the gallant French, salutations. There shall arise one day the poet who shall sing of their deeds in words of fire. We can but lift our hats to them and say "Well done!"

Everyday Heroes of the R.A.F.

By Hamilton Fyfe

It was the second day of the Battle of St. Quentin, September, 1918. In a sector near Bullecourt our troops were just holding their positions. They could not hold them against heavier attacks. What we wanted to know was whether the enemy was about to make his attack heavier. The only way to find out what he was doing was to send out an airman to see. Off he went—or, rather, off they went, pilot and observer—and came back very soon to say that about three thousand Germans were massed in a sunken road, evidently waiting to advance. It did not take our artillery long to get on to that sunken road. High explosive bursting in it, shrapnel bursting over it, made it an inferno.

Those Germans did not advance. They retired.

That illustrates one of the immensely valuable activities of the Royal Air Force. Our airmen all through the difficult days of the offensive brought in day by day regular and accurate information as to the enemy's formations. I have seen them flying in weather which seemed both too wet and gusty for flying, and too thick for any useful observation to be done. On such days they took chances by flying very low, and many times they came back with news which enabled our commanders to stave off fierce onslaughts which the Germans meant to be a surprise for us.

FRONT LINE IN THE AIR

In the battles round Morris and Bailleul the British air scouts kept our commanding generals fully informed about the enemy's concentrations. Often we broke up these concentrations, and prevented attacks from developing against our tired troops. The wind was high, and driving rain-storms blotted out every now and then the ground on which the straining eyes of the observers were fixed. Yet hour after hour they went up, and saved us from many a surprise which might have had baleful consequences in that time of touch-and-go.

They took part themselves in dispersing enemy forces gathered for attack. They flew low and dropped bombs. One officer came into a headquarters where I happened to be one morning, and announced that he had "let go" from a height of not more than a hundred feet on a party of Germans whose number he put at 400, and had made "a good hit." They also flew down and machine-gunned the enemy on the roads. Earlier in the battles we owed more than can be said to

136

the airmen who harassed the Germans by these means on their way through the Somme country.

At one moment it is scarcely an exaggeration to say that the Air Force was holding our front line. Early in the last week of March, when our Third and Fifth Armies were so hardly pressed, the German reinforcements were flowing through Bapaume and Albert and along the good main road—good because we had kept it in order—which runs through those little towns.

Orders were given to the Air Force to attack them as vigorously as possible, with the object of checking their advance and gaining time for us.

By the energy with which they carried out this order, the flying men made that main road too dangerous for the Germans to use. First, they dropped four tons of bombs on it while infantry were on the march. Then they swooped down to within less than a thousand feet of the ground, and used their machine-guns. There is no more terrifying experience than being machine-gunned from the air.

Harrying the Invader

Those Germans who were not hit ran for shelter, crouched in ditches by the roadside, glued themselves to the trees that shaded it. For the time being that road was made impossible for the enemy to use. The columns of relieving troops were sent round by small by-roads.

Transport columns could not travel anywhere but on the good roads. These our airmen continued to strafe. There were some terrible scenes on those days. Wounded horses screaming, others bolting as the reins fell from the hands of their lifeless drivers, waggons blocking the road, dead and dying men in heaps almost. Both by day and by night the long files of lorries, vans, and carts, which are the necessary accompaniment of armies, were harried from above. The difficulty of regularly feeding the German soldier was doubled.

I went one night to an aerodrome to see a bombing squadron start on one of these expeditions. One after another in the darkness the big machines, their engines roaring, rolled off their marks and slid into the air. ft was all done so quickly, and so much as a matter of course, that one hardly thought of the errand on which all these young men were bound being dangerous.

At dinner they had been chatting and chaffing, just like any other young officers who might be going to spend the evening quietly in their mess. Then they had gone out, inserted themselves into their flying suits, climbed into their machines, all with such an air of habit, as mechanically as a motor-driver climbs into his car. They were not in the least excited or disturbed.

FLYING HEROES

Yet every one of them was risking his life in the most perilous way or, to speak more correctly, ways. There was not only the possibility of the machine coming to grief in the air; or the chance that a bad landing in the dark might turn it over and kill the pilot. There was the danger from the numberless "Archies" and machine-gun batteries which would try to bring the bombers down. One of them had been telling me how it felt to be followed by the searchlight, and to know that a quantity of tubes were spitting death at you.

It is not true that our airmen feel no apprehension when they are being shot at. Those who suggest this show their ignorance of man's nature and do the Air Force poor service.

It is because they do feel it that they deserve, every one of them, the highest distinctions for valour. And all the more when one considers how effective their action is upon the enemy. We captured a young sergeant in May, well educated, and a candidate for a commission. He knew what he was writing about, and his diary, which he had kept up to the date of his capture, was the finest testimonial that British airmen could desire. Almost every day he records "Air raid. Bombed by aeroplanes. Took refuge in cellars." He mentioned the losses suffered, an ammunition store blown up. One could read how the spirit of the German troops was being lowered by the nightly visits.

Of the adventures that our pilots have had in the air there are enough to fill a book. The coolness and pluck which they show when their machines are damaged, and when it depends upon their nerve whether they can escape with their lives, are beyond all words of admiration. Take the case of a man whose machine was hit and set on fire. He dived from the height of 15,000 feet, at which he had been fighting, intending to land if he could get down quickly enough. But as he went, he tried to put the fire out and, marvellous as it sounds, he succeeded.

Then, instead of landing, he went to the assistance of a comrade who was being hard pressed by several German flyers. His engine was giving trouble now, and his Lewis gun was jamming, but he drove the enemy off, and both got safely to earth, though the partially burned machine caught fire again and became a total wreck.

For some time, few Germans came over our lines. I can remember weeks in which I saw none at all. An Air Force major determined to taunt them with their unreadiness to take up our challenges to fight. He flew over one of their aerodromes and dropped a parcel in which he had wrapped a pair of boots, with a note to the effect that they were for use on the ground, since the German airmen had ceased to fly. It would have been rather a heavy joke if that were all. But the real point of it came when the major flew back while his parcel was being examined and dropped a hefty bomb!

As a rule, the Air Forces of all the warring nations show a good deal of chivalrous fellowship to one another. Thus, the Australians, who cannot be charged with treating the enemy too gently, gave the crack German flyer Richthofen a military funeral, and put an inscription on his coffin calling him "a valiant and worthy foe," and other flying units sent wreaths for the grave. I went to this funeral, and thought it a very noble and generous manner of burying a brave enemy. I was sorry to see protests made by people in England. Such protests, I am sure, found no sympathy from the troops in the field.

Those who sit in armchairs and foam at the mouth upon the slightest provocation would be surprised if they heard the language soldiers use about them. They spoke their minds on this occasion, as my ears can testify.

Some Interesting Anecdotes

VICTORIES OF THE GREAT FRENCH AIR FLEET

None of the sensational expectations of the destructive action of aircraft has yet been fulfilled. Half a dozen huge German Zeppelin airships are reported to have come to grief—some destroyed by the high-angle fire of the allied armies, others wrecked by defects of construction or handling.

The bombs dropped by German airmen have ruined a few peaceful buildings in Belgium, but when launched at troops in action they have done less harm than a shell from a quick-firer.

On the other hand, the French fleet of the most skilful and daring airmen in the world has already rendered services to the Allies of the highest importance. It surpasses all that General Joffre and his staff hoped for. The French airmen have become the lightning messengers and marvellous eyes of the allied armies. They fly at a height where they are completely out of range of the new Krupp aerial guns. At the altitude at which experience has taught them to fly their vision is perfect.

1: THE MARVELLOUS EYE OF THE ARMY

Nothing—absolutely nothing—escapes the trained eyes of the observing officers. They are even able to count the exact number of trains in a German railway-station, the number of carriages on the trains in motion, and distinguish the units—infantry, cavalry, artillery—of the hostile armies marching on the frontier.

Not the slightest tactical movement of the enemy escapes their notice. For instance, early in August one of the French airmen made an aerial raid of 250 miles. He saw and reported the whole immense movement of German troops from Metz and Treves to Aix-la-Chapelle.

The General Staff of the allied armies know every daylight movement among the masses and skirmishing lines of a million and a half Germans and Austrians.

In the meantime, the Teutonic airmen were trying to carry out the same work of inspecting the arrangements of the allied forces. But their Zeppelins are practically failures, and their aeroplanes are not properly built for observation work. The disposition of the engine, especially, on German flying-machines prevents the observing officers from seeing exactly what is directly beneath them—from having a direct, perpendicular vision of the allied armies. The Germans have to peer ahead and look over the side of their machines. Owing to the obliquity of their field of observation they can see at a height of 3,600 feet only what an allied airman could see by direct vision at a height of 7,200 feet. The mist troubles them, and veils the details of the Allies' movements. This is one of the reasons why the French were so successful in surprise attacks in Alsace and Lorraine.

Resourcefulness sometimes introduces an element of humour into the most perilous situation. A French airman, losing his way in a fog, came down to find himself in enemy hands. The German officer got into the machine, and holding a pistol to the head of the airman, ordered him to reconnoitre over the French trenches. The Frenchman perforce complied, but when over his own lines he suddenly proceeded to "loop the loop," with the result that the German of-

Letting Him Down; French Pilot's Expedient

ficer, who was not strapped in, was tipped out, while the resourceful French airman flew cheerfully home, to be mentioned in despatches and decorated.

2: Triumphs of the French Aviators

This, however, does not mean that the German scouts of the skies are quite negligible in comparison with the craft of the Allies. Their machines are clumsy and difficult to handle, and their airmen are somewhat too careful of their own safety; nevertheless, they are rendering certain services to the German War Staff, though much inferior to those rendered to the Allies by pilots full of dash and resource, who are every day performing astonishing exploits.

The first fortnight of the war was extremely precious to the French airmen. In a few days, in a fever of creative work, the French did more to improve their military aviation than they had done in two years. The brilliant French genius for improvisation was soon as the best. And soon every morning the allied airmen utilised all they had learnt the evening before, and the armies of freedom fight under the direction of squadrons of flying men, armed and furnished and organised with the efficiency of the British Armada in the North Sea. The airmen carry orders from the General Staff to all the different units, inform the commanders how their orders are being carried out, and watch over all the movements of the enemy.

Brtain Gaining Mastery of the Skies

Sir John French's despatch of September 11th, says:

One of the features of the campaign, has been the success attained by the Royal Flying Corps. In regard to the collection of information it is impossible either to award too much praise to our aviators for the way they have carried out their duties or to overestimate the value of the intelligence collected.

General Joffre values our aviators, too, and has written complimenting them.

During a period of twenty days up to September 10th, a daily average of more than nine reconnaissance flights of over 100 miles each had been maintained. The object of our aviators has been to effect the accurate location of the enemy's forces, but when hostile aircraft are seen they are attacked instantly with one or more British machines. A good many German pilots or observers have been shot in the air and

CAPTAIN GERARD RESCUING AN AVIATOR'S MECHANIC FROM UHLANS

their machines brought to the ground. The British Flying Corps has thus established an individual ascendancy which is as serviceable to us as it is damaging to the enemy, who have become much less enterprising in their nights.

Bomb-dropping has not been indulged in to any great extent. On one occasion a petrol bomb was successfully exploded in a German bivouac at night, while, from a diary found on a dead German cavalry soldier, it has been discovered that a high-explosive bomb thrown at a cavalry column from one of our aeroplanes struck an ammunition waggon. The resulting explosion killed fifteen of the enemy.

DARING RAID ON DUSSELDORF BY BRITISH AIRMEN

Before the war armchair critics of the British War Office condemned in unmeasured terms the supposed laxity in making proper provision for an effective military aeroplane service. Yet a few weeks after the war opened, we read with pride and admiration Sir John French's despatch of September 11th, where he said:

> The British Flying Corps has succeeded in establishing an individual ascendency which is as serviceable to us as it is damaging to the enemy.

The raid on the Dusseldorf Zeppelin sheds, announced by the British Press Bureau on September 23rd, was the first great feat of aerial daring of which we had information The weather was misty, but in spite of difficulties of pilotage, Flight-Lieutenant C. H. Collet approached within 400 feet of the Zeppelin sheds and threw three bombs. His machine was struck, but he was unhurt, and he flew back over 100 miles to his base without having had to touch earth during the double journey.

Captain Gerard is one of the most daring of French military aviators. After scouting near Compeigne he brought his Caudron biplane down rather near the German advance posts, and the *Uhlans* made an effort to surround him. He had to rise in the air, leaving his mechanic behind.

A military car is at the service of every aviator, and carries spare parts. In this case Captain Gerard's car came up, and its crew went to the rescue of the abandoned mechanic. There was a pretty skirmish between the *Uhlans* and the aviator and motor crew. All the French party escaped unwounded, but two dead *Uhlans* were left behind.

The Zeppelin sheds at Dusseldorf upon which three bombs were dropped by Flight-Lieutenant Collet in the course of the daring air raid made by officers of the Royal Flying Corps, who gave proof of their superiority over the German aviators

Daring Airmen of the Friedrichshafen Raid

The "record" feat of aerial daring was the work of three Englishmen—Squadron-Commander E. F. Briggs, of the Royal Naval Air Service, Flight-Commander J. T. Babington, and Flight-Lieutenant S. V. Sippe—who, on November 23rd, penetrated one hundred and twenty miles into German territory, across mountainous country in difficult weather conditions, and made a bomb attack on the Zeppelin workshops at Friedrichshafen, on Lake Constance. These workshops were a source of great pride to the German nation, because they were erected by national subscription to enable Count Zeppelin to pursue his work in airship construction when disaster seemed to be pursuing his efforts with disheartening persistency.

The Germans had been informed by telegraph of the approaching airmen and bombarded them with guns, machine-guns and rifles, but, notwithstanding this, they flew down to striking distance and launched their deadly missiles.

Squadron-Commander Briggs was a victim of this German fire. His petrol tank was pierced, and he was thus forced to volplane down to earth, but as he passed over the objective building, he continued to drop bombs. He was wounded, but not seriously, and captured on landing.

His two companion adventurers succeeded in flying back to their base, and asserted positively that they achieved their purpose the destruction of the Zeppelin and the Zeppelin shed. Officially, the Germans denied that this result attended the raid, but non-officially the British claim was confirmed.

At the request of General Joffre all three airmen were awarded the Cross of the Legion of Honour.

Britain's Surprise for "Wideawake" Cuxhaven

It would be interesting to know how Admiral von Tirpitz felt on learning of the intrepid British seaplane raid on Cuxhaven. The gallant admiral had just been giving expression to some delightful braggadocio schemes of waging a really ruthless war and torpedoing Britain into starvation.

As if in answer to his fatuous threats seven naval airmen, assisted by the light cruisers *Undaunted* and *Arethusa*, destroyers, and submarines, attacked the Huns' torpedo station on Christmas Day, dropping bombs with deadly precision on ships at the Elbe estuary. The outstanding features of the exploit were the evasion of the enemy submarines for three hours, through skilful seamanship, and the utter futility of what Germans considered their trump card the Zeppelins. Two of the latter were engaged, but soon turned tail and fled.

This, the sixth successful British air raid on German positions, was unique in that submarines, surface ships, and hydroplanes worked for the first time in unison.

While Tirpitz was trying to make the flesh of his foes creep by bombastic talk, daring British airmen acted, not however on an undefended seaside resort, but on a centre bristling with every danger from land, sea, and sky.

The Great Air-Fleet Raids on the Belgian Coast

The British Navy of the Air did some particularly brilliant work. Never before had so many machines acted in unison as when, on February 12th, 1915, Wing-Commander Samson, the Nelson of the Air, led thirty-four aeroplanes and seaplanes in a great attack on German submarine bases. Although flying part of the time through a violent snowstorm, and exposed to heavy fire, not a participant was injured.

The only accident was the immersion of Flight-Commander Grahame-White in the sea off Nieuport. An even more ambitious expedition took place four days later. Forty Allied aircraft dropped 240 bombs on German positions in the same districts. Eight French aeroplanes took part in this magnificent exploit of aerial warfare.

The Fokker and Other Items of Aerial Interest

After eighteen months of warfare, the European campaign seemed definitely to have settled down into a drawn game. Neither side appeared to have realised its original plans to any great extent. Millions of men were involved, but one group of antagonists could not claim any great superiority in manpower.

It became more than ever a duel of intellect. Some new invention, some wonderful aeroplane, some amazing gun, might turn the balance completely in favour of one side or the other.

The Germans adopted the Fokker aeroplane, which proved itself efficient for what is known as "barrier" work, or keeping the Allied machines from the German lines and obtaining information. It remained for the Allies to find a challenge to this effort of enemy engineering.

CAPTAIN AND FLIGHT–COMMANDER ALBERT BALL, D.S.O.

With the Royal Flying Corps Zeppelin Strafers

Both on the west front and at home our aviators established permanent ascendancy over the enemy. The fact that by October 1st, 1916, four Zeppelins had been brought down in England was calculated to induce the Germans to modify their policy of frightfulness, in spite of the ravings of Count Zeppelin. This notorious German found it increasingly difficult to justify his hideous invention, and one which had cost his Fatherland several millions—to no real military purpose.

It is significant that where competent German reconnaissance was most needed, on the Somme front, it was conspicuously unsuccessful. Certainly, no Zeppelin dared appear over the Franco-British line. That is why Paris was immune from the couriers of hate, and, with the perfection of London defences, the Zeppelin found it increasingly dangerous to approach the British metropolis.

Our Star Flyer: The Hero of a Hundred Fights

Captain and Flight-Commander Albert Ball, D.S.O. Sherwood Foresters and the Royal Flying Corps was the champion airman of Britain during 1916. This young officer gained the Military Cross and he had been awarded a bar to his D.S.O. He was regarded as the "star flyer" at the Front, and accounted for about thirty enemy machines, and never a Hun plane winged over his sector without finding him a ready and formidable antagonist. On one occasion he observed twelve enemy planes in formation, dived in among them, and fired a drum into the nearest machine, which went down out of control. Several more hostile machines then approached, and he fired three more drums at them, driving down another out of control. He then returned, crossing the lines at a low altitude, with his machine very much damaged.

Captain Ball, who is the son of a former Mayor of Nottingham is only twenty years of age, and prior to 1916 had had no experience of flying. It is said that his favourite device is to manoeuvre beneath his enemy and then empty a round of ammunition into the German's petrol tank. Although he has had several narrow escapes, Captain Ball has never been injured. He is described as a "short little chap, with longish black hair and eyes like a hawk, he goes to battle in his shirt-sleeves.

Leap for Life from an Observation Balloon

The work of the men in observation balloons along the battle-front was of the hazardous nature. Each observer has a harness of webbing about his body and thighs. To this a strong cord is attached,

Leaping from a damaged observation balloon. The observer has to jump clear instantly. His fall releases and opens the parachute, which permits of a gradual descent. Above: Two observers descending by parachutes from balloon set on fire by an enemy aeroplane.

and should his balloon be hit or break loose from its tether with a prospect of drifting over the enemy lines, the observer throws out his charts, books, and instruments, and instantly drops out of the basket. When he has fallen the cord's length, the pull releases the parachute, neatly folded in the case alongside the basket, which at once unfolds and steadies his farther descent.

Should the balloon be at a good height it may take the parachutist as much as ten minutes to descend.

Our Allies' Wonderful Machines

The famous types of Italian and French aeroplanes proved of great service—the small "Spad" as a fighting machine and the giant Capronis for their carrying capacity.

The Caproni triplane is worked by three 600 h.p. engines, has a speed of over eighty miles an hour, and carries a ton and a half of bombs.

The Caproni biplane, which possesses great lifting power, carries two pilots, a gunner, and an observer, as well as a considerable load of bombs.

CAPRONI BOMB–CARRYING BIPLANES CROSSING THE MOUNTAINS.

These machines which were extensively employed by the Italian Air Service, carried out successful raids on the Austrian naval base at Cattaro. They carry large loads of bombs.

LEONAUR

ALSO FROM LEONAUR
AVAILABLE IN SOFTCOVER OR HARDCOVER WITH DUST JACKET

WINGED WARFARE *by William A. Bishop*—The Experiences of a Canadian 'Ace' of the R.F.C. During the First World War.

THE STORY OF THE LAFAYETTE ESCADRILLE *by George Thenault*—A famous fighter squadron in the First World War by its commander..

R.F.C.H.Q. *by Maurice Baring*—The command & organisation of the British Air Force during the First World War in Europe.

SIXTY SQUADRON R.A.F. *by A. J. L. Scott*—On the Western Front During the First World War.

THE STRUGGLE IN THE AIR *by Charles C. Turner*—The Air War Over Europe During the First World War.

WITH THE FLYING SQUADRON *by H. Rosher*—Letters of a Pilot of the Royal Naval Air Service During the First World War.

OVER THE WEST FRONT *by "Spin" & "Contact"* —Two Accounts of British Pilots During the First World War in Europe, Short Flights With the Cloud Cavalry by "Spin" and Cavalry of the Clouds by "Contact".

SKYFIGHTERS OF FRANCE *by Henry Farré*—An account of the French War in the Air during the First World War.

THE HIGH ACES *by Laurence la Tourette Driggs*—French, American, British, Italian & Belgian pilots of the First World War 1914-18.

PLANE TALES OF THE SKIES *by Wilfred Theodore Blake*—The experiences of pilots over the Western Front during the Great War.

IN THE CLOUDS ABOVE BAGHDAD *by J. E. Tennant*—Recollections of the R. F. C. in Mesopotamia during the First World War against the Turks.

THE SPIDER WEB *by P. I. X. (Theodore Douglas Hallam)*—Royal Navy Air Service Flying Boat Operations During the First World War by a Flight Commander

EAGLES OVER THE TRENCHES *by James R. McConnell & William B. Perry*—Two First Hand Accounts of the American Escadrille at War in the Air During World War 1-Flying For France: With the American Escadrille at Verdun and Our Pilots in the Air

KNIGHTS OF THE AIR *by Bennett A. Molter*—An American Pilot's View of the Aerial War of the French Squadrons During the First World War.

AVAILABLE ONLINE AT **www.leonaur.com**
AND FROM ALL GOOD BOOK STORES
07/09

LEONAUR

ALSO FROM LEONAUR
AVAILABLE IN SOFTCOVER OR HARDCOVER WITH DUST JACKET

THE FALL OF THE MOGHUL EMPIRE OF HINDUSTAN *by H. G. Keene*—By the beginning of the nineteenth century, as British and Indian armies under Lake and Wellesley dominated the scene, a little over half a century of conflict brought the Moghul Empire to its knees.

LADY SALE'S AFGHANISTAN *by Florentia Sale*—An Indomitable Victorian Lady's Account of the Retreat from Kabul During the First Afghan War.

THE CAMPAIGN OF MAGENTA AND SOLFERINO 1859 *by Harold Carmichael Wylly*—The Decisive Conflict for the Unification of Italy.

FRENCH'S CAVALRY CAMPAIGN *by J. G. Maydon*—A Special Correspondent's View of British Army Mounted Troops During the Boer War.

CAVALRY AT WATERLOO *by Sir Evelyn Wood*—British Mounted Troops During the Campaign of 1815.

THE SUBALTERN *by George Robert Gleig*—The Experiences of an Officer of the 85th Light Infantry During the Peninsular War.

NAPOLEON AT BAY, 1814 *by F. Loraine Petre*—The Campaigns to the Fall of the First Empire.

NAPOLEON AND THE CAMPAIGN OF 1806 *by Colonel Vachée*—The Napoleonic Method of Organisation and Command to the Battles of Jena & Auerstädt.

THE COMPLETE ADVENTURES IN THE CONNAUGHT RANGERS *by William Grattan*—The 88th Regiment during the Napoleonic Wars by a Serving Officer.

BUGLER AND OFFICER OF THE RIFLES *by William Green & Harry Smith*—With the 95th (Rifles) during the Peninsular & Waterloo Campaigns of the Napoleonic Wars.

NAPOLEONIC WAR STORIES *by Sir Arthur Quiller-Couch*—Tales of soldiers, spies, battles & sieges from the Peninsular & Waterloo campaings.

CAPTAIN OF THE 95TH (RIFLES) *by Jonathan Leach*—An officer of Wellington's sharpshooters during the Peninsular, South of France and Waterloo campaigns of the Napoleonic wars.

RIFLEMAN COSTELLO *by Edward Costello*—The adventures of a soldier of the 95th (Rifles) in the Peninsular & Waterloo Campaigns of the Napoleonic wars.

AVAILABLE ONLINE AT **www.leonaur.com**
AND FROM ALL GOOD BOOK STORES
07/09

Milton Keynes UK
Ingram Content Group UK Ltd.
UKHW021807141024
449461UK00026B/102/J

9 781915 234162